A New Leaf

5

ALSO BY JIM GOLD

BOOKS

Songs and Stories for Open Ears

Handfuls of Air: A Book of Modern Folk Tales

Mad Shoes: The Adventures of Sylvan Woods:
From Bronx Violinist to Bulgarian Folk Dancer

Crusader Tours and Other Stories

RECORDINGS

World of Guitar
American Folk Ballads

A New Leaf

5

Adventures in the Creative Life

❧

Jim Gold

FCP

Full Court Press
Englewood Cliffs, New Jersey

First Edition

Copyright © 2005 by Jim Gold

Published in the United States of America
by Full Court Press, 601 Palisade Avenue,
Englewood Cliffs, NJ 07632
fullcourtpress.com

ISBN 978-1-946989-53-6
Library of Congress Control Number: 2020904310

Editing and book design by Barry Sheinkopf

Table Of Contents

Writing, *1*

Languages, *7*

Life, *12*

Money and Its Brethren, *93*

Performance, *103*

Business, *133*

God, *179*

Inventions, *183*

Writing

Big Question

I'm in Prague with nothing on my mind.

I just changed the font size but the screen size didn't matter. Something is wrong here, but I don't know what. I'm totally bored with my writing. Am I at an ending? My writing is at a standstill. Where to now?

Should I move into a third person voice? Or write about history?

The emotional need to express myself in the first person, *New Leaf* style feels repetitive. And yet, I know no other way.

Where do I go from here? Do I even write at all? And if I do, what will I write about? In what style? In what voice? Or have I said everything I need to say?

Should I go back to children's stories and fables?

Yes, where am I going from here?

This may be the big question of this tour.

Chronology versus Categories

I am considering editing my own *New Leaf.* This is a major step forward!

Now I can personalize the book even further. And answer the big question: Chronology versus categories. Barry believes in categories. Minimal categories. . .only six of them. . . but categories, nevertheless.

In my gut, I have never believed in categories. *New Leaf* is more real in its chronology. After all, that is the way it happened. It is the development process laid out exactly the way it happened, just as it unfolded in my mind.

Now is my chance to think about this deeply again. . .and, through my own editing, act on it!

Accepting Passion

Why write? Because I must. I enjoy it.

Why publish? Because I must. I enjoy reading my writing.

I may develop a small audience of fans. Or I may not. The main thing to remember is I enjoy reading my writing. My sense of humor is a blast as is my sense of beauty. As I reread Mad Shoes, Crusaders Tours, Handfuls of Air, Songs and Stories for Open Ears, what fun! What an off-beat sense of wild imagination!

I love reading what I write. That is the real and only bottom-line reason to publish it. It is based solely on my enjoyment. Just as others follow me when I enjoy my folk dancing, so they may enjoy reading the books I write. Or they may not. They may buy them. . . or they may not. But, bottom-line, I must enjoy them. Truth is, I do. I just have to recognize and admit it.

Passion, luxuriation, and enjoyment are forms of love. Before I can love others, I'd better love myself. Before I can love editing or publishing, I'd better love the process of editing and publishing.

Dubrovnik

I edited the Dubrovnik portions of my *New Leaf.* In the process, I started practically rewriting the entries using new language, and new poetic forms.

In the process, I realized that this was a way I could actually edit my pages. . . by changing them, transforming them, metamorphosizing them. In other words, my editing was not necessarily dry editing but actually hanging new words on the old skeleton, using the skeletal *New Leaf* form to create a new poetic work. I could also add foreign words and Joycean babble writing in the process. I could, actually create a new language, my own language, perhaps incomprehensible to others (or less comprehensible), but mucho fun for myself. Such a new language, new poetry, new form would move me beyond *New Leaf!*

"I Wonder If. . ."

Early morning writing is "I wonder if" time.

I like to wonder. . . especially early in the morning. Let's look at the phrase:

"I." Easily related to the ego, the self that is writing.

"Wonder." This word is the key. A wonder is a miracle. Looking at the early morning world in awe and wonder, seeing it as miracle. Not a bad way to begin the day.

"If." This word speaks of future possibility; what might happen. Certainly a good partner with "wonder."

Summing up: Early morning "I wonder if" time is a fine way to begin the day.

This meditative wonder, as expressed through attitudes, styles, and movements, get more concrete as the day moves along.

Editing as Deepening

I am now editing to deepen my writing.

In the process, I clarify and sharpen my thinking. This is personally helpful. It also reminds me of the importance of written thoughts.

If they are important to me, they will also be important to some others. They key word here is "some."

For "some," a select few, reading these written thoughts will be vital.

Although difficult to acknowledge and remember, this fact shows the importance of publishing . . .no matter what!

The Fifty-Year Perspective and Practice

George Bush has said, "The history of my administration will be written and understood in fifty years."

This is also true of my *New Leaves*, and my others books. Therefore, they should be published with this long-term perspective in mind. They are being written to handle the present, but being published for the future, for future generations, for my children, and my children's children.

I am so focused on the present it is difficult to see the importance of what I am doing.

Developing a long-term perspective, fifty-years (as least) would be a very good practice.

Fine-Tuning

Reading *New Leaf 3* in the morning is better than reading someone else's work. As I reread, I fine-tune.

Fine-tuning is a better word for me that editing. I hate editing! But I don't mind fine-tuning at all. In fact, I like it! Its like perfecting a guitar piece; I play it over and over again, for weeks, months, years, and, in the process, I make tiny changes and "improvements." Fine-tuning can be fun.

Clarity and Brevity

I called Barry for his thoughts. He said: In the editing war between ego and insight, aim for clarity and brevity.

Editing Fun!

What is my personal test on "good editing?" How can I tell if I'm doing it right? What is my bottom-line emotional—and even intellectual—standard?

Editing has to be fun!

To my surprise, it is slowly becoming that way. I'm enjoying reading and believing what I've written.

Art, Artists, Soul. . .and Marketing

The trip to the library taught me something. After I searched and found the books on marketing on the Teaneck Library shelves, I felt nauseous. When I took them out and gave my card to the librarian, I felt disgusted. As I drove away with them in my car, I felt empty.

Finally, when I read, or rather, "glanced" through them at home, and felt totally bored, I realized I would never read them. Next day I returned them to the library, went down to the shelves on Artist Lives, and took out books on Rubens and an autobiography on Thomas Hart Benton. The Benton book is great. I can't put it down. How did he live? How did he make it and get along? How did he "market" his art and survive in the art world? Plus I am sympatico to him as an artist. How do artists survive, inspire, and get along? Here are subjects I am vitally interested in. Books on lives of the artists: These are real books on marketing!

Preparation, Editing, and Publishing *New Leaves*

Visiting Eleni was good for me. She is not publishing her best historic work on economics, banking, and perhaps the Ottoman Empire, she is not realizing her personal dream, and neither am I. I encouraged her to publish. I also face a own publishing problem. Am I now ready to encourage, nay insist, that I prepare, edit, and publish my own works, my own New Leaves?

Why would I do this? Why put in so much work, if there are no public rewards up ahead, no sales. Why pile up more books in my basement? Why put in all this work "for nothing?"

Maybe I should do it because editing, preparing, and publishing all the Leaves of *New Leaf* is a Kantian good-in-itself.

It also has cosmic significance: Writing and publishing my works is one of the reasons I was put on earth.

These are two fundamental truths. By not plunging into this necessary, but often distasteful, preparation, editing, and publishing work, I open myself to the overwhelming, cosmically depressing feeling that life is purposeless, directionless, and meaningless. This feeling is, indeed, a killer. Since I prefer life over death, by fighting to prepare, edit, and publish New Leaves, I am actually fighting for my life! I am choosing life over death! A wise choice, indeed.

The very fact that cosmic depression consumes me when I do not write, or not work to fulfill my dreams, demonstrates that I'm on the wrong track, or rather, no track at all. Lost without purpose, wandering trackless and without energy, in a desert of meaninglessness.

There "is no choice" for me. I must prepare, edit, and publish all my New Leaves. It is part of my central life's work. I will not be satisfied until it is done, or at least until the task is tackled. As Jews say at Passover, "Although we may not complete the task, we must constantly work towards liberation."

Self-Publishing, Book Promotion, and Creative Marketing

Went to Carol Lutchen's talk on self-publishing. Very good. Two things took place in my internal brain.

1. Embarrassed when she mentioned my name as "the famous Jim Gold" As she kept praising me in public, as a writer, self-published writer, folk dance teacher, traveler, and business man, I kept blushing.

Am I ashamed of myself as a writer. . . and all else? Was I not prepared for the "public assault" on my person? And this, even though it was all praise worthy? If I am ashamed of myself as a writer, and ashamed (or afraid) of what I have written, wouldn't this certainly slow down even prevent sales?

Good questions. But I'll look into them later. Besides, they may simply be remnants of my old self, the one I am leaving behind in my post-transitional period. My new me, the gone-public me, the one that lives on promotion, sales, and gone-public, is called, rather than surviving in a "Death of a Salesman" mode, now thrives as a Perpetual Salesman self.

2. I also realize my time to promote my books is not yet. Total sales focus is now on tours.

But I feel deep with my bosom, that focus on book sales is coming. . . perhaps post-tour season, in the fall. . . .

This will include upgrading my book (and CD) web site, listing myself on Amazon.com (ask Carol about how), and in other, at the moment, unknown ways. I'll focus on a creative marketing approach.

Languages

Paean to Pain

If in the history of the French language, stress led to the reduction to shwa of Latin post-tonic vowels, then what is stress doing to my body? Is it reducing my "post-tonic vowels," in their form of loose ideas, wandering thoughts, rough imaginings, to a stronger, more stable architecture, a more focused and concentrated power of mind?

Is the stress of a touring life as expressed in the jolts, bumps, pointed, jumpy, and jumping pains in my body, forcing me to focus more clearly? Are they pointing me in a more unitary, solid, focused, and powerful direction?

Certainly, this would be a positive view of the function of pain. Pain focuses the mind. . . and quite clearly.

Is the cosmic purpose of these pains to increase the power of my focus, and, in the process, concentrate my mental powers on my true purpose(s) in life?

Indeed, this could be viewed as a pain *b'simcha* approach. The pain of cutting off vague unfulfilling directions helps to increase focus in one direction.

Does pain ultimately increase focus on a greater good than the pain itself? Or is it simply a pain in the ass?

Visceral Linguistics?

I'm trying to memorize the French word "blafard" (pale, wan, livid). I realize as I search for synonyms, memory devices, part of me is saying: Why bother? Why make the effort?

After all, how important is learning an insignificant word liked this?

In fact, how important is learning French or any foreign language for that matter? Truly, I can get along without it. I can function and survive without French. Maybe my life will be richer with it, but truly, bottom line, who needs it?

If part of me is thinking these killer, deadening thoughts then no wonder it is difficult for me to memorize words, learn foreign languages, and, in general, make an effort, give it my all.

Why bother?

I still don't have an answer. But until I do, I will continue to study languages "half-way" and half-assed. I don't like to study that way.

But my attention will remain divided until I heal my internal linguistic "Why bother?"

I don't feel a visceral need to learn languages. The effort is not like music or the arts, or even the study of money. Or is it? Perhaps it is quite visceral. Only I don't see it yet.

On the Linguistic Understanding of Computer Language

Evidently, I can only understand computers, electronics, and even science only on a poetic level. That's why I have to look up the origins and etymologies of all words used: microprocessors, buses, digital, analogue, etc. In order to understand the concepts behind the language, evidently, I have to dream and wander through the words.

Thus I connect computer study with my love of language. Specifically, it means looking up computer words in both the *Webster New World Dictionary: College Edition* with its etymologies and word origins, and Isaac Mozeson's *The Word,* with its etymologies and words origins based on Hebrew roots.

From Mozeson's book, I would move to the bible, the *Tannach,* to find the Hebrew roots of words and their poetic etymological origins.

In the beginning, computer study with its movements into the fields of electronics, physics, mathematics, chemistry, and science was unconnected to anything else in my life. Now, however, it has been reconnected to my linguistic love, my love of music and sound, and thus to my soul.

I wonder if my left shoulder pain was related to this computer disconnection. Now that I have reconnected will the shoulder pain go away? We'll see. But deep in my heart, I have confidence that it will!

The progression goes from computer language to etymologies to Hebrew word origins to the Bible to love of music and finally, to feeling and immersion into the Beautiful Vibrations of Sound.

Touring the Scientific Universe

This scientific voyage may not be a one-year detour, but rather a permanent shift in the direction of my psyche.

It may be a trip into the future by returning to the past. After all, I did start college as a physics major. I wanted to understand the romance of the universe.

Now that I have toured the artistic and cultural universe by developing myself as an artist, and, through my tour business, visited many countries, perhaps it is now time to shift my vision, my development and direction, and start touring the scientific universe.

"Science" from Latin *scire*, "to know" (and Hebrew *sakhel*, says Mozeson, with its relationship to words like skill: Old Norse, *skil* (reason, discernment).

Saxon: *Knife*, cutting, separating.

Hebrew: *Sakhel*: Mental discrimination.

What is science but knowledge with different spelling.

Rubato Guitar. . .Leads to a Rubato Life

I just looked up the word "rubato." It comes from the Italian "robbed." I rob pieces of tempo and expression. Rubato has an outlaw quality, a bit of the rebel, too. Doing things "my way." Robbing the past to feed the present. I like it.

Only Bulgarian

Now I will be reading only Bulgarian until my tour to Bulgaria this August. Well, when I was nineteen, in France I read only French for a year.

When I started the tour business twenty-two years ago, I focused only on Hungarian for a year. Hungarian language, history, culture, everything Hungarian. After going through my transitional year, I am returning to past forms.

This is my Bulgarian year. Everything Bulgarian. Starting with language. In my life, it's return-to-past-forms and consolidation time. I see it as lasting three to five years.

Life

Web Sites and Internet

The world of web site and internet is opening up.

I'll explore and contact links to Hungary, Spain, France, Norway, Sweden, and Greece. I'll contact others, link to their pages, create new pages of my own based on interests like language, classical guitar, writing, examples of my writing, yoga, running, and folk dancing.

This is about passion, the passion of learning, expansion, and growth, the passion about getting more.

Dribbling Away

I woke up with an unusual pain on the inside of my left knee. I interpret it as a new form of "folk dance knee."

Also my body and I feel stiff and rigid; it resists movement in a loose and fluid manner.

I am at some kind of stationary, resting place. A rest-and-resist place. Good description. As I rest, I resist. What am I resisting? Is it the feeling of growth, expansion, ecstasy, jubilation, appreciation for my accomplishments?

It could be. I "don't know what to do" with these feelings. They are similar to the intense feeling of peace and inner satisfaction I felt after my program/concert/appearance at the Hidden Children Hanukkah Party. What a great success that was. Inner glow, satisfaction, and peace, a quiet ebullient happiness over a job well done.

What do I do with such a feeling? In the past, I would simply get a headache, and that would be that. By the time the headache ended, I had forgotten the feeling.

What do I do with such a feeling now?

One answer is: Feel it.

Suppose

Suppose I need only minimal warm-up on guitar. . . or even none? Or am able to get warmed up during my first slow and easy piece.

Suppose it is the same for folk dancing, yoga, and running too (start with a micro-running warm-up).

Could that be the reason I am doing no running, yoga, or even guitar practice? That I no longer need it? Maybe it has become like singing. I never practice singing, or even need to. I remember all my songs, and, after minimal (even no) warm-up, can sing them in public.

Maybe the fruits of all this training and practice is that I no longer need training and practice. Maybe I now know it so well, totally, and deeply that further practice and training is unnecessary.

Suppose this is also true for organizing and running my weekends, tours, and even doing bookings like bar mitvahs.

Suppose, I am at the point where, in order to maintain my skills, I really have to do nothing. Or I need only do the absolute minimum.

Is this my new place?

Reflections on the above written on the following day: The answer is "No!" Proper warm-ups on the guitar, all the legato, scales, and arpeggios done for about fifteen minutes minimum; half hour is better. It can and should also include "Alhambra" and "Leyenda."

The old way of playing with the old order, like the old miracle schedule, is right. I must maintain my skills. How is that done? If I do nothing, they will, no doubt, deteriorate. Therefore, I have to do something. What? The minimum. What is the minimum? How little must I do to maintain my skills? And, if I practice not at all, in other words, do nothing, will my skills really deteriorate? Or will they, like singing, remain the same, that is, go nowhere?

I believe, or want to believe the latter. Do nothing, and my skills will remain the same. I want this because, deep in my heart, I have no motivation to merely "maintain" something. Create or destroy is my motto. It is dynamic. Mere maintenance is enough to motivate me to do anything.

But I am in a maintenance mode. . . and probably will stay in this state of suspended animation, until a better idea comes along.

Revolution

What is a revolution but a turning around, turning over, turning upside down.

The idea that notes are secondary is totally radical and revolutionary. It turns my "Alhambra" on its head.

Excitement: A New Year's Gift

I taught dancing for New Years First Night in Teaneck last night. It's the first time I've taught or even folk danced since we went to Santa Fe.

I felt nervous before my teaching (a good pre-, per-teaching nervousness. It made me feel alive!

Pre- "anxiety" makes me feel alive! Time for a verbal change. Leave out the prefix "pre."

Use Energizer, Uplifter, Excitement. I like them.

I think Excitement is best.

Victory!

The process of writing is frustrating and painful.

Yet it is better to write than not.

But a creative cloud descended upon me.

It started Wednesday afternoon when I said "I deserve a vacation." But it didn't fully hit until Thursday when my stocks started to slide; Friday they collapsed, setting me back a few thousand dollars and putting me almost back to where I was at the end of December. I was down several thousand in December, up several thousand in January; now I'm down again. All this market effort has left me nowhere.

Why am I down? It's partly related to the stock market merry-go-round, but not completely.

Most is because of victory!

Success makes me sick. But I also love it.

If I have been down, my victories can tell me why. Let's look at them.

First comes the title of this *New Leaf* itself: Passion! It is the leaf after and beyond New Adventures. Adventures take you somewhere. Passion means you are there. No place to go. Firmly rooted in the present. Success in guitar playing. Look at the victorious words to describe my new musical place: "Sweet, Mellow, Sensuous, Sensual, Luscious, and Beautiful." If that is not a victory, I don't know what is. It tells me I can apply these new "guitar rules" elsewhere in my life. I can focus my passion on business and my miracle schedule.

Other victories: 1. Publication of Volume 2 of A *New Leaf*. I've been very cool towards this victory. Why? I don't care to discuss that now. But it's true, nevertheless.

2. Computer. My lessons in web design, internet promotion, and computer knowledge are paying off. Victory afer victory, win after win. I feel comfortable and am actually starting to understand codes! Or at least, I am developing a desire to understand. A new field and direction in learning is opening up. I am slowly mastering Fidelity Active Trader Pro and Dreamweaver web design programs. Enthusiasm and joy in curiosity are victories here.

3. Stock market. Well, strangely and believe it or not, I have to include it. How can this be a victory if, in a mere three days, I've lost all my profit? Well, it is a victory of attitude. I am not panicked by my Triquint losses. I feel partly "I've been through this before." One can make or lose lots of money in the market in a few days. I've done both. I am frightened and annoyed. . . but not panicked. That is progress.

Because of these losses, I developed new attitudes towards the market.

Short selling. Can I learn how to handle a down or up market and, hopefully, even make money in it? That would be major learning. Also there is the philosophical, gut wrenching—acceptance of up-down cycles of life reflected in market cycles. Can I flow with them? In this sense, the stock market becomes my teacher.

These are positive attitudes towards adversity. They help me deal with challenges, overcome difficulties, handle the miseries and afflictions of life.

All victories. Instead of clamping down on enthusiasm, denying the glory of victory, refusing to gush with joy, I will now leap out my door, charge down the street, and shout "Wahoo!"

And that will be another great victory!

Resistance!

Knees, ankles, shoulders, and back are stiff with resistance!

What do they resist? Mostly, the outward social and people activities. And yet, part of this is energizing. Part of me loves it.

Conflict and rubbing.

Will I always resist? Will the only place of comfort always be the inner chamber of Imagination, the teenage room at home in Riverdale? Maybe.

Can such a room ever become totally available in public? Or will there always be an element of defense against the outer forces of negativism?

Can one ever be comfortable in public? Will I consistently be threatened when I socialize, meet others, or perform? Will I always resist?

Will such resistance always be "expressed" in bodily aches and pains, stiffened lower back or joints? Is this the stiffed-necked, Jewish resistance?

Freedom through defense may be a good and necessary thing. It saves and protects the center, the spiritual core.

Thus, I ask: Is my body really falling apart? Or is it being fine-tuned to resist? Am I a resistance fighter belonging to a long line of ancient freedom fighters? Am I ever fighting for my right to be me?

There is also the fact that I have been in a social straight-jacket this entire week of Florida Folk Dance Camp and "vacation." Soon it will be over. I can't wait to get home!

This whole week was a big success.

My next challenge is: How to handle success, its pressures, tensions, responsibilities, life style, joys, defeats, and victories.

A post-Florida Folk Dance Camp door is opening. New questions and challenges are coalescing: How to deal with and handle success.

It means doing yoga with a new success attitude.

It means playing guitar with a new success attitude.

It means walking down the street, carrying luggage to the car, going to the airport, and more. . . all with the new success attitude.

Not being so disturbed by idiotic liberalism is also a victory.

("Liberalism" is a perversion of the word "liberal," itself a perversion of the meaning of liberty). I brush it off now. I am solid and confident in my views of freedom, individualism, dignity, tolerance (in the old sense of the word), and self-worth. Modern liberalism consists of dried up Soviet regurgitations. It is "communist state control lite," dictatorship gone soft. Nevertheless, thanks to our founding fathers, they have a constitutional right to idiocy.

I see a war with Iraq as one of liberation. On the deepest level, America is performing a public service.

No "liberal" would want to live under Hussein, or the old Soviet Union either. But they can criticize the United States and its love of freedom from afar. It's fun because they are safe. Unlike Iraq, or the old Soviet Union, where you would be tortured and sent to prison for expressing opposing thoughts, here they have no price to pay for their views.

Beyond Books

No book can tell me about the relaxation, strength, and spiritual beauty I discover while playing the guitar. These feelings, thoughts, and ideas are not in books. I alone can delve into this secret of self.

The next step is beyond books. A personal, in-depth study. Entering deeply into my mind, I travel to places never seen before. No outside person can lead me there. Segovia and his ilk are out. I alone can only discover the shivers of this North Pole or the heat of its Equatorial Jungle.

I am on an expedition into the molten center of my being. It consists of white-hot passion, ice-cold calm, barren and luxuriant fields and valleys.

Beyond books I sink into the Mystery.

Strength and Clarity; Confidence and Illumination

Crack through old habits. How about playing the Villa-Lobos "Prelude Number 4" arpeggio fifty times.

Wow, now that's different! Can I do it?

1-10. . .to 13: The warm-up period. Soft, mellow, slow.
13-17. . . Strong, somewhat slow.
17-20. . .Faster, strong, and clear.
20-23. . Strong and clear. . . but not fast.
23-27. . . Slow, stronger, and clear.
27 onwards. . . (slow), stronger, and clearer.

What are the values implied in this practice? Slow or fast may be valuable but they seem are not values.

Strong and clear are values. "Strong," implies confidence. "Clear" implies illumination.

"Fast" and "slow" are servants of strength and clarity, of confidence and illumination.

My conclusion after playing Villa-Lobos' "Prelude No. 4" arpeggio thirty times:

Practice for strength and clarity; confidence and illumination.

Passion Explorations

Am I willing to take the passion change and jump into passion?

This new leaf is called Passion! But feeling passion, doing passion, living passion is very different from merely writing the word.

Start with guitar. How do I express passion playing the arpeggios in Villa-Lobos' "Prelude Number 4"?

By playing over the sound hole I now create "Sweet, Mellow, Sensuous, Sensual, Luscious, and Beautiful" tones. This is a technical change. But it is not passion.

Passion involves taking a "dive-right-in" chance.

Taking one means I might miss notes, makes mistakes, mess up before God and man. But the Mystery of passion's energy would be released. That is the glory and terror of passion.

Returns

I continue the study web site design and stock market trading.

Runs: I have committed myself to daily morning runs. (I am "aiming" for a marathon by October of 2004.)

Writing: I have committed myself to daily writing.

Tours: I've sent out all my ads. I've entered all descriptions and key-words for my web site. I still can make calls.

Folk dance classes: Nothing more to do but show up, and give great, high-energy classes!

Weekends. Make some calls.

Klezmer Bookings: Bar and bat mitzvah dates, weddings. Let Michelle handle them.

World of Jim Gold concerts: I'm rewriting publicity copy. I'd like to promote these concerts. But I don't know where and how yet.

Book Promotion: This can be promoted through my concerts, web site, Full Court Press, and public readings. But although writing is central to my life, promoting my books is not. Or at least is not yet. We'll see where this leads.

Joy in Disguise

Excellence is my dream. Have I stopped striving for it? If I have, it explains my listlessness, my lassitude, and fatigue. By celebrating the wahoo of success too long I have relegating Becoming to the back seat.

Time to move on.

To what?

A higher level of suffering? Yes!

Dreams of excellence are dreams of expansion. Suffering while striving to reach a higher goal is a joy in disguise.

Return to Science Through the Mystery of Numbers

There is "artistic truth" in charts and in Leonardo Fibonacci's ideas, too. I like numbers. I especially like the mystical idea of numbers as expressed by Pythagoras. Imagine tying my fascination with kabbalistic mysticism to numbers and the stock market.

As I child and young man I liked numbers and science. This interest was expressed by choosing physics as a major in the University of Rochester. It inspired my dreams of the universe. Then came low

marks on tests. Slowly and gradually, love of physics, science, numbers, and mysticism was drained out of me. I had never heard of
mysticism. At that time, science and mysticism were then on opposite
side. I never knew I was a closet mystic and that Beauty, with its mystery, was one of my core values. I dreamed away in private. Slowly
physics and all interest in science dribbled away.

But perhaps now I can return through the mysticism of Fibonacci
numbers. . .and their "practical" application in the stock market.

Secret Beliefs. . . Money

In the past, I couldn't admit confidence in predicting the future.
Who am I to predict it, anyway? What audacity! say it. But deep
down, I always believed it.

But secretly, inwardly, I had nerve and audacity. Look how I dared
conduct the Music and Art orchestra, go to France, become a social
director at Chaits at age nineteen, dared to make a living as a guitarist,
embrace the entrepreneurial life, lead tours to foreign lands. What
nerve, indeed. Yes, chutzpah and daring. All hidden behind a smile.
Even going into debt implies daring. I dared put my finances on the
line because I believed in myself and that, in the end, I could and
would pay it all back. So many things I do and did point to daring,
nerve, and audacity. I just never dared to tell anyone about it. Going
public with my self-belief would lead to the verbal smack of "Who
you? Ha!" So I hid behind a smile.

But secretly, I always knew.

Now I admit it to myself...and publically.

See Through Clouds

Should I look with wary eyes upon hope? Isn't the Henry Miller
hopelessness ("I have no hopes; I'm the happiest man in the world"),
a form of living without expectations, a good place to be?

Why bother with hope in the first place? Why not live in the present,
do what I have to do in the best way possible? That, after all, is the bottom line: Focus on doing the best I can, and the hell with the rest.

Optimism

No matter how bad things appear, I always seem to come up optimistic. I wonder why.

This shows how vital dreams are. Crushing them means crushing life itself. That is why hope-crushing is so devastating. If I let fear win, if I give in to the hope- crusher, and, in the process, give up my dreams, I am dead. That is why I end up on the side of optimism. Even though it is often "unrealistic," it at least means I will live. Perhaps that alone is enough to make it more realism than pessimism.

What is more real, life or death? Well, truth is, both are real. Sometimes life wins, sometimes death wins; sometimes optimism, sometimes, pessimism, sometimes hope, sometimes fear. But whether I want or need them, they are nevertheless, there to deal with forever, representing my struggle with the opposites, the daily challenge of dialectical existence, the endless battle of life.

Metaphysical Doorways

There is magic and mystery at transition points.

Doorways are their symbol.

This is true in sales, too. You put in the conscious calling and advertising. Then suddenly, mysteriously and magically, someone registers!

Your effort is the commitment part. Once the commitment is made, then, mysteriously, Providence steps in to help. These are the magic transitional points of metaphysical doorways.

The Gospel of Enthusiasm

This is my "St. Paul" period of life. I'm delivering my gospel. Paul had total belief in his cause and what he was doing. Like him, only total belief in what I am doing will sustain me. The core of this belief is enthusiasm. "En theos," in God, en-theos-iasm.

What is my calling?

To bring enthusiasm to myself and the world.

Only enthusiasm will lift me out of my seat, move me out of the house and into the world, force me into public places to proclaim the Good News.

Believing I'll Win

In the past, I approached most situations with two contradictory views: one of confidence, the other of fear and trepidation. One was a stimulant, the other a brake.

These contradictory beliefs served to cancel energy. I ended up partly paralyzed. Only when I finally arrived at running the event was I pushed into a more confident mode.

Why did I cancel out my energies? I'm not sure. And, at this point, I don't even care. All I know is that phase of life is over. I'm through with division, contradiction, and fighting the inner battle between confidence and fear.

I'm moving on to a belief in the ability to win.

The Power of Ideology

Ideology is a fragile and illusory wall of protection against new thinking.

It acts as a defense against daily, fresh and fluid visions of the world. Ideology protects the fragile ego but hides the true self.

It is based on fear of freshness.

And builds a barrier of protection against excitement and revelation.

And makes one narrow and constrained.

Ideology gives the illusion of safety. But it creates nothing except walls.

You and I

New Leaf is about me and you. Otherwise, why would you be reading it?

A dream is a liquid form of the future.

Gabriela, our Czech guide, said: "The Czechs in Prague, although mostly Catholic, are tolerant but not religious. It is said they go to church only three times: for hatching, matching, and dispatching."

She also said: "Middle age is when a broad mind and a narrow waist change places."

Play with the pain. A most important concept!

Is yoga an art form?
Is calligyoga an art form?
Why not make it one?
Calliyoga is my invention, my art form.

Our Hungarian guide, Adam Molnar, said:
"Why is there no terrorism in Hungary?
Because our buildings fall down by themselves."

Renewal

What is Hungary's eternal truth throughout its vicissitudes of history?
Renewal.
The ever-fighting human spirit constantly fights for renewal of itself. The flow of renewal is the historic process itself.

History of Freedom

Does the flow of history lead anywhere? Yes. Towards greater freedom. No matter how often people get knocked down by wars and destruction, they keep rise again, fighting for their freedom.

Somehow the soul's innate desire for freedom never dies. Nor can it ever get killed or destroyed. It keeps popping up, searching, trying, renewing efforts to realize itself in the fullness of freedom.

The story of my soul is the story of its struggle to grow, expand, and fulfill its potential. It is the story of a struggle to be free.

The history of my soul mirrors the history of mankind.

When imagination and dreams become "concrete" they metamorphose into business, calls, and sales.

Post-Transformation Me

Imagination and dreams gone public are sales. They are the gospel in business form.

Can studies be a part of this? What about art? Have they turned into sales forms? Yes.

Dreams, imagination, business, and art merge into gospel. A lifetime conflict has disappeared.

Confidence and Celebration

Why is it important to convince others to see my view of reality?

Sure it's nice to celebrate agreement with others. But why do I need their support? After all, celebration is celebration. It could be just as much fun to celebrate alone.

On the Pluses of Opposition

It is hard to believe that opposition to my views will never go away. . . ever! True, some people may change their mind and even come over to my side. But opposition to views will always exist.

There is some good in the existence of such an opposition.

1. Opposition dispels blandness.
2. Opposition puts pepper into the food of political life.

Creativity

An artist
Cannot be afraid to jump
Off a cliff
Into the dark, churning abyss;
To fall down, down, down

Into black, mysterious waters
And drink from turbulent streams
Of Creativity.

I Need a Cloudburst Miracle

I am stuck. That may be the reason for the sudden appearance of all these new-place pains. Look at them: elbows, wrists, fingers, knees, insteps, and probably more upcoming, too.

Arthritis is a stiffness of mind expressed through stiffness of the body. Only a cloudburst of creative rain will heal aching joints and muscles.

This miraculous lifting of pain comes with a dynamic new idea, a flash of fresh vision.

I wait one eagerly.

The Center

Maybe once you've reached the center, there is no place else to go. You enter the home of the Higher Power. You have arrived. When you come home, where else is there to go?

Starting Over Based on Passion!

In the third century B.C., what motivated Pytheas, the Greek navigator, to leave Marseilles? Business and sales. He went northwest to investigate trade routes, to the amber and tin markets of northern Europe. On the way, he found Thule, or Iceland.

History is Alive and Well. . . Always

Ma nishtanah? What is the difference between history and the present, between characters of old and characters of new?

Not much.

Thus when I read about history I am really reading about family relationships. Isn't Abba Abraham part of the family? My father and Abraham of Ur. Isn't David part of the family? King David and my son David?

Indeed, all are One.

The great secret is that history is a study of the present. Its characters are alive and well. . . always.

Sheer Delight of Study

I read and study not so much to remember or improve but rather for the sheer delight of hearing the words bounce around in my brain and ricochet off the walls of my mind.

Sheer delight is close to Godliness, to the Shining, the Radiance, and the Great Unnamed.

Losing is the Best and Only Lesson

Arrogance is based on an unreal sense of self, an inflated sense of power.

Stupidity often leads to arrogance.

How to you learn the lessons of arrogance?

You lose.

Losing, although painful, is the best lesson.

"Can" and "Will"

Can I have more energy by eating carefully?

Will I have more energy by eating carefully?

Can or will: What is the difference between these words?

"Can" has possibility. It derives from the Anglo-Saxon word *cunnan*: to know. (German: *kennan*; English: *knowledge*). Thus "can" as in I can do it means I know how to do it. No learning is involved since I already know how to do it. However, I still have to use my will power to motivate myself to do it.

"Will" has intention and rational power: "I will do it." It comes from an Indo-European root wel: to wish, to choose.

Cry for Beauty!

What is the meaning of the headaches I often experience during my Weekends and Tours?

The pain results from a repression of ecstasy, the overwhelming inner wave of cosmic Beauty that sweeps over me.

I cry for the beauty of these events.

Winning and Losing

Winning creates fun;

Losing creates resolve.

How does the above apply to me?

See body pains as losses. They strengthen my resolve to cure them through by running, doing yoga, etc.

Missing the folk dance steps are losses. They strengthen student resolve to master these and even more steps.

Missing "alhambra" tremolos and arpeggios creates resolve to master them.

Customer rejection creates resolve to get more customers.

Stock market losses create resolve to master emotions of greed and fear, and to make money in the market.

Losing stinks.

That is why it is so energizing.

Demands

I am demanding of myself. I demand my best effort.

Would I dare demand this from others?

Would I dare demand they strive, push, sweat, and struggle, and give their all in the pursuit of perfection?

This changes the nature of my sales calls. Rather than coaxing, cajoling, convincing, pleading, asking, nay begging them to dance, come on tour with me, or whatever, I am now demanding they do so. . .for their own good!

This demand will be subtle, of course. It may take the form of a persistent or subtle "insistence." But it will be a demand, nevertheless.

When I lead dancing at Bar Mitzvahs, weddings, or special events, I do not request that people dance. I do not ask them to dance. Rather I say: "Let's dance!" I demand it (subtly, of course.) I do it with presence and through voice tone.

On "Moderation"

Man needs a little defiance of conditions in his life. Otherwise he will be killed by boredom.

The road to ecstasy is the road of boldness, daring, adventure, and creativity. It is the path of heroes and daring deeds.

During the past few months, even the past year, tempered by losses in the stock market, I have tried the road of "moderation."

Well, this road sucks. It is not my deepest nature to follow the straight, flat, boring road of moderation. I thrive on a path of sharp curves, rugged mountain peaks, and deep twisting valleys.

Some might call this path one of stupidity. But I call it the path of wisdom.

Why? This path may open the door to ecstasy. Ecstasy in turn will cure my aches and pains. In fact, maybe I had those aches and pains in the first place because I had traded it in for tight-assed, straight-jacketed, nauseating and disgusting moderation. In other words, much of my energy went into keeping myself back, putting my brakes on, holding myself down, repressing my wild and ecstatic energies, and swallowing the best of myself. No wonder I felt like throwing up so often; no wonder I felt like shit and was plagued with an almost constant disgust.

Moderation is just not my way. I admire and love artists, wild men, passionates, and fanatics. Does killing yourself lead to ecstasy?

Yes. But you can only do it once.

Energizing Myself

I'm afraid if I exercise too much, I'll get tired and injure myself. But suppose if I exercise too much, if I over do it, instead of becoming tired and injured, I energize myself. That's possible too.

Could my biggest fear be I will energize myself! And, bottom line, what does energize myself mean? The very real possibility of touching Passion! and ecstasy.

Rather than something to fear, this is something to embrace!

Giving it my all, rather than tiring me out, releases endorphins and energizes me!

As for over-use injuries, the best defense is self awareness.Life

Politics and the Divine

How do political leaders fit into God's plan? Are they "chosen" by God. Often they use religion to empower and rationalize their reigns. Nevertheless, just because they use the name of power of God in vain does not mean that God has not chosen them. Someone has to run a country just as someone has to run the universe. And since God is the Big Guy, wouldn't He chosen "smaller potentates" to run his worldly fiefdoms? Why not?

Prophets, wise men, and mystics often believe that God's plans are revealed to the special few through revelations. Why wouldn't some of these revelations be political? Why shouldn't their power be tied to political power?

Yes, politics and the divine are related. Only I am not yet sure how.

Dynasties rise and fall. They exist in the material world and are thus subject to the vicissitudes of life. But daily changes in the dream of this material world are all connected to the great Unchanging.

Material life is a dream but the infinite, eternal, and unchanging Truth is a Reality.

No doubt, miserable and slimy as it often is, politics is connected to the divine.

People are outwardly, secretly or even unbeknownst to them, looking for their God connection. Often they place it in other humans, so-called "leaders."

When they mistake their leaders for gods, they commit idolatry.

When they realize their leaders are symbols, means, bridges to the divine, but not the divine itself, they are closer to enlightenment and true divinity.

The process of looking for a leader in yourself, but making the mayic (illusionary) mistake of looking outside yourself, "finding" it in someone else, a so-called "leader," goes on throughout history. It continues until self-realization.

On a secret level, the political leader who will someday come has many names in many languages. In English he is often called the Messiah. He will create peace on earth. Mystically, this means he will create peace in the warring human soul. Indeed, a difficult task.

The human soul is ever at war with itself. These wars are reflected and "expressed" in the political battles and military wars in the theater of ever-changing history.

Let Them Suffer

Through their attitudes, people create most, if not all, of their own suffering. They do this in order to learn about the nature of life and the meaning of their existence here on earth.

Since this is so, why should others work so hard to relieve their suffering and pain? Suffering is their creation. Isn't it arrogant and cruel to take their creations away? Why not let them suffer and learn in peace?

Of course, if they ask for your assistance, that is another story. But most of the time people don't want or ask for your help. Usually they suffer silently and "in peace." Subtly and secretly they know this is how to handle and figure out the solution to their problems.

Let them suffer. Why take this vital source of learning away?

Life of Study?

Am I looking for the simple life of withdrawal and study?

This would entail teaching of folk dance classes, running one or two tours a year, one or two weekends, and scattered bookings.

The simple life would give me the time and space to study.

What does my post-transformational heart want? That is the question.

Devotion to a life of study is a type of retirement. My type.

But would I miss the entrepreneurial excitement, the ups and downs, of running after people? Probably.

Brief Disguised Return of the Old Neighborhood

Meeting Rama at Barnes and Noble opened the door of the past. I started to flirt with the repressions of the old neighborhood. Soon I downloaded all the information on the breatharian, Shri Hira Ratan Mankek.

Reading about his breatharian life style soon began to depress me. It gave me the perfect philosophical excuse and reason (as does the vacant, empty, removed feeling of the witness state) to return to the old neighborhood, and, in the process, kill my desire for a Passionate life style.

Morning Downs as a Hidden Fresh Energy Source

Each morning it is a question of starting all over, starting fresh, trying to get in touch with my energy base. Just because I write about it in my books, and even put "starting fresh" in my *New Leaf* titles, does not mean I have a permanent key.

Each day I start off as a virgin.

Right Elbow Awareness Day

Notice how my right elbow started to hurt as I wrote the above entry.

Could my elbow pain be my "modern form" of resistence to wanting more? I've understood my other resistence forms, back pain, knee pain. I've even made progress on understanding instep pain. But right elbow pain? Up until now I have not been able to figure it out.

Self awareness has helped me close off my mental exits to wanting more. But new resistence forms ever rise in their place. Could my right elbow pain be such a form? Indeed, it is possible.

Sleep

I am "falling asleep" during my fast tremolo.
Sleep is the rock of resistence to fear.
Fear is the gateway to energy. The door of sleep closes off fear.
Mine is the sleep of resistence.

On Wild Energy

On Thursday morning I ran one hour and twenty-minutes.
I ran fast. I "over-ran."
What does "over-ran" mean?
I entered the wild. . . and I got a bad cold with sniffles, fever, and a cough. I still managed to teach folk dancing Friday night in Goldens Bridge. I gave it my all, too. Got home late and went to bed at three a.m. I woke up with a sore throat Friday morning. It was downhill from there.

What is the moral of all this?

I entered the wild. . .and I got sick. I entered that land of raw, dynamic, wild emotions, I broke all barriers, I let out the wild flow. . . and I got sick. Did the wild flow make me sick? Or was it my resistence to it?

If the power of the wild flow can make me sick, can its power also cure me? Can I burn away my diseases, swallow sickness in wild flames of flow?

Why not?

If an excess of energy made me sick, why can't an excess of energy cure me?

Try it and see.

This time when I ran I gave it my all. The release of wild energy into my system did not

Last week I had been frightened into sickness. Was it less threatening to get sick than face the awesome power of released wild energy?

This energy is hot, fiery, and dangerous. If I'm not careful it could destroy me.

Was a part of me "wise" to get sick, and thus protect myself?

On the other hand, I want to be in touch with this wild energy. I want to use it, and not get sick.

How could that be done?

Awareness would be the first step. Focus and meditate upon the wild energy within me. Visualize it, witness it. Then use it.

Bursting Through the Disease Wall: Release of the Wild-Energy Self

I'm so mad about this cold! I can't shake it.

This anger is releasing wild energy on the guitar. I'm flying across "Alhambra", "Leyenda," "Alard," "Zapateado," and "Bulerias."

Is my anger, my rage at this head cold breaking down the wall between my wild energy and my guitar playing?

Is it part of the universal plan to release my imprisoned wild self?

I am studying about Iceland. Soon I'll be traveling there. What does this approach to "all things" have to do with the Alþing, the "All Thing, the General Assembly, the eleventh century Parliament in Þingvellir (Assembly Plains, Parliament Plains) Iceland?

Is my trip to Iceland about to open up a new form of wild glacial energy? Glacial because my breakdown started with a cold.

As I fulminate, twist, and scream in my sneezing prison, even my lower back is hurting. This is rage at its best!

The nature of mind is to ever do battle, and be buffeted about by conflicting ideas. Monkey mind jumps. Attention scatters in all directions and runs wild.

We struggle tame it. No wonder we need sources of self-soothing.

Loving my Fear: Seeing its Beauty and Wisdom

I worried that by being successful I would lose my fears and thus an important source of motivation.

Ha! What a joke! Although I have passed through my transition, I still have all my fears. True, some old ones have gone away. But new ones quickly came in to take their place.

I breathe a sigh of relief. Fears are great motivators, and without them I feared I would lose my motivation. Thus, fears of fear bred lack of fear, which in turn bred more fears over lack of fear.

This means I can be successful and still keep my fears! They do not depend on success or failure! Win or lose, my fears will never go away. Thank God!

Imagine, part of me spent thousands of dollars on therapy and years of hoping I would somehow be able to cure myself, rid myself of my fears.

Well, indeed, I would be free. Free of motivation, free of wanting more, free of all hopes and desires, and, along with that, free of the desire to live. Who needs or wants such freedom?

I want my freedom to include the freedom to fear. And it does!

I love my fear. I see its beauty and wisdom.

Iceland and Beyond

Imagine, I am now sitting in Stockholm, the original home of the Vandals!

The Next Wild Step: Finding your Inner Troll

Could wildness return?

How about in writing. . . or my exercises?

Could I "wild" a bit further?

Notice, I do not say "push." There is a difference between "push" and "wild."

What is it?

"Push" tries to improve. Part of it still tries to please the public world.

"Wild" tries to plug into the inner wild man who is crazy and, yes, divine. I need to be in touch with divinity. But I need a new, post-transitional term for it.

Can wildness return—in writing, exercises, and yes, even the rest of my miracle schedule?

Is that what this Scandinavian tour is all about—the rediscovery, on the next level, and return to wildness?

Well, the best way to return is to start today. Now.

Presently, I have writing, exercises, and study. All are members of the miracle schedule. Notice I have combined running and calliyoga into the term "exercise." I don't like that word. Maybe I can find a better one. But the development, the idea of combining them is good. It is another step towards unification and a wild All-Is-One.

I can begin by ever remembering the little troll within.

What is a troll? Could such a mythological figure become my next wild word for divinity?

Study mythology. . . start with Nordic mythology. Fairy tales and fables. Personal mythology expanded and going wild as I search for a new term for wild man.

One thing about the troll within: it is wild and scary; it lives and thrives in darkness. It retains its power in caves but turns to stone whenever sun light shines upon it. Just as light kills darkness, so it may turn my inner troll to stone. Evidently, great powers dwell within the kabbalistic darkness of fear, dread, and panic. These represent the black side of challenges living in caves or at the bottom of the abyss. The inner troll can ride wildness into a fiery hell of laughing challenge.

What is the troll philosophy? Turn your living hell into a laughing challenge! Let your dark abyss feed a bottomless adventure!

Work and Vacation

Without work, I fall into a funk. My inner self becomes lost, energyless, discouraged, and then rapidly frizzles away.

I need work at all times. . . even on "vacation." For me there really is no such thing as a vacation in the traditional sense of the word. I hate the idea of stopping work; I hate the vacuum and emptiness that the traditional idea of "vacation" creates. Get away from it all? Who wants to get away from something I love?

Not I. Change yes, vacation, no. That's my motto.

In light of this love of work idea, what should I do about our upcoming "vacation" trip to Canada?

First, do not think of it as a vacation. As of today, give up all noxious ideas of vacation, cutting back, and getting away. These notions are terrible for my brain. The best I can do is think of the upcoming trip to Canada as a working vacation.

What is a working vacation? It boils down to simply working in another location. I've built my life around having my own personal vacation twenty-four hours a day. Canada will be no different.

What work shall I bring to Canada?

All work: Writing (my computer), running and yoga, of course. Language study: French (and Greek). And stock market books.

For me, work and vacation are synonymous. Thus when I run I am going to work; when I do yoga I am going to work. Running and yoga are part of my work. Studying languages, or anything else, is part of my work. Playing guitar and singing are part of my work. Sales calls, running tours, writing and sending out ads are all part of my work.

All my work blends together into one great Work. And that Work is called Vacation. Capital letters say it all.

I can't stand lack of structure. But I also hate it when others try to impose their structure upon me.

Best for me is to impose my own structure upon myself.

I ran beautifully yesterday. An hour and a half, much of it in fast mode. I also added a phenomenal meditation: I turned each physical pain in my body into a miniature stimulus packet. Instead of mentally avoiding pain, denying it, trying to get past it. I looked directly into its face, saw it as a hidden, kabbalistic energy package, a stimulant delivered to me in pain form. Slowly, mentally, by visualizing it thusly, the pain did not only go away, but turned into a stimulant! What a wonderful way to view pain!

Also by seeing running as part of my work, I turned it into a job, my job, my calling. It rose in importance and slowly became part of All-Is-One.

This important idea is part of the post-Icelandic, post-transformational life. My miracle schedule activities are no longer separate from so-called outside life. They now belong to All Is One. Miracle schedule vacation time has turned into work time. . . and vice versa.

New Views of Pain

A pain appears under my left knee cap during the slow squat. Reinterpret it as a hidden center of energy, an energy packet located under my knee cap.

Focus on this pain as energy packet. See it slowly dissolve. As it does, my interpretation of it as pain, disappears. Then watch the pain turn into energy.

An Hour a Day

An hour a day spent on anything is a lot. Especially if you do an hour a day for many days, months, and years. It creates a considerable skill.

All I seem able to do is a hour a day. (And this not even on every day.) An hour a day is usually my limit.

Thus I may be able to fit in lessons in computer, languages, gaida, and even accordion.

There's also the idea that one skill enhances and feeds the other.

Cosmic Sadness is the Creative Call

The cosmic sadness is the creative call.

It tells me I am not paying attention.

In the world of creativity things rarely "go well." Creativity is gutsy, heart-breaking, dynamic, wild, disorderly. It is full of storms and unruly passion. It is the call of the wild sounded from deep within the heart.

Give up ideas of order, calm, and even happiness. These pills of mildness can never cool the inner cauldrons; they cannot stop the internal eruptions of volcanic creativity. Nor should they. Staying in touch with the demonic power of the unruly mountain god, bursting through the illusory crust of calm, personal civilization, the soft-iron mask of habits, customs, schedules, and routines.

The steam-roller juggernaut marches out of the inner cauldron; wild fires and molten lava stream down from the mountain crater. There is no stopping the burst-through maniacal marching-mouth of Creativity.

The morning sadness I feel is the cry of Life bursting through my stagnant head. Thank God for the passion-reminding, life-giving, cosmic-enhancing sadness. Without it, I would be a dead-head, crushed-hearted, undulating corpse.

The Gift of Maximum Effort

The gates of heaven open when you make the maximum effort. Energy flows through your being. Aches and pains, worries and frustrations dissolve as you surrender to the higher power.

This momentary but wonder-filled state of wisdom, peace, and composure is the gift of maximum effort.

Rather than avoiding, distancing yourself, running away, or retreating from aches, pains, frustrations, and worries, the best way to handle them is: Work harder! In the heat of battle you discover amazing strengths!

Slightly Hard

I need to do things that are slightly hard. Too hard, I get discouraged; too easy, I get bored.

Slightly hard is just about right. It inspires me to make maximum effort.

Greece: Cretan Quest

I want to come back from Crete with more than language control and some dances. . . although that would be good.

Better, best, would be to return with a new attitude.

This morning I read a quote by Patrick Leigh Fermor in Yvonne Hunt's excellent book *Traditional Dance in Greek Culture*: "Nowhere in Greece (more than Crete) is the quality of *leventeia* so clearly manifest. This attribute embraces a range of characteristics: youth, health, verve, high spirit, humour, quickness of mind and action, skill with weapons, the knack of pleasing girls, love for singing and drinking, generosity, capacity to improvise mantinades. . . and flying like a bird in quick and violent dances. Levanteia often includes virtuosity on the lyra: it is the universal zest for life, the love of living dangerously and a readiness for anything."

At this moment in my life I am looking to rekindle the love of living dangerously. Obviously, it includes a readiness for anything.

Sacrifice your ego on the altar of others.
Why "sacrifice?" Because it hurts to give up the ego.
What are the rewards for this pain?
Self-transcendence.
That what business is all about.
And marriage, too.

Taking care of others, trying to figure out how to make their tour better, belongs to the metaphysics of fun. It's fun to care for others.

The opposite of impatience is not patience but taking the long term view.

If life is about more than money and business, maybe my folk dance teaching is too. But if it is, can I afford to spend so much time doing it? If I do, I'll have to accept a life of poverty. Poverty itself may not be so bad. Some think it is a laudable, desired state, especially for religious people or ascetics. Maybe my calling is one of artistic riches but financial poverty. Instead of wealth, think poverty. If I do, then teaching folk dancing for almost no money is right in line. So are most of my other artistic endeavors. This way of thinking might even cause me to give up the miseries of the stock market.

Perhaps my goal should be to accept and try to live in poverty. This way of thinking might even give me more peace of mind.

Moving Forward by Going Backward.

I am waking up with strange, old-time, cosmic depressions. This has not happened for months, years. It has not happened since I discovered and followed my miracle schedule.

But for the past few weeks, I have not followed it; I have been abandoning it in favor of much and many "detail" work projects: Preparing for Florida Folk Dance Camp is the main one—and this entails, of course, learning several new music recording and CD creating computer programs. Added to this, on the side, is my new Address Organization, Quark, Dreamweaver and Photoshop (in the distance) programs.

But mainly, it is the Music Match (and Pyro Cakewalk) CD creating programs that consume me.

This along with reorganizing all of my folk dance tapes, CDs, and records, and all of my international songs.

Thus there is a tremendous reorganization going on coupled with a computer learning process. I have been feeling overwhelmed by it all and have given up my daily writing. Thus, depression.

What to do?

Obviously, the best thing is to return to morning writing, as I am doing now. Even as I touch my morning fingers to the keyboard, I start to feel better; as the words pour out, the fog and veil slowly lift. It always feels like a miracle. And it is!

No question I need morning miracles to light my day. . . and my life. Submerging their light, fire, and spark beneath the burden of future progress only serves to shove me in a hole, smother my jumping joy, snuff out the light, remove me from God's graces. Yet when this happens, as it has been happening during the past two weeks, what can one do? Probably follow its misery until the bugger has run its course. Well, the course is almost run. It is a new week. We'll see where all this leads.

I must return to my miracle schedule. It has always worked in the past; it is working now; and, I'm sure, it will work in the future. It has always been my path to growth, satisfaction, inner revelation, and self-understanding. There is no reason why this should be any different today. Indeed, I am moving forward by going backward.

Fear of Death

Whenever fear of death comes along, with its concomitant meaninglessness of life and purposelessness of striving for more, think of reincarnation, and the eternal union and unity of God's Spirit.

Does reincarnation exist? Does it really take place? I cannot prove it. I really do not know. But I do know that the beautiful concept and stellar idea of reincarnation give purpose, meaning, and unity to my life. Thus I need it. Does needing it make it true? Probably.

Chasing Away Old Man Pain

Why did ninety per cent of the pains in my shoulders "suddenly" and "miraculously" go away? Posture correction? Doing a one-and-a-half hour total yoga session? Both? Other? Could that have been "all" I needed? Are, or were, other psychological factors involved, such as the overwhelming computer learning I had to accomplish during the month of November? It's true that, during this time, I gave up total focus on all my miracle schedule, heavenly exercise programs— yoga, running, and the 50s. I hardly even stretched after folk dance. Nor did I warm-up before dancing. It was all part of an experiment to see how little I can do, how much I can get away with before such physical neglect created the inevitable slow decay of my body.

I'm not sure about the answers to these questions. But it sure is nice to be ninety-eight percent pain free for awhile.

Notice how, after most of the pain drained out of my shoulders, I awoke with a sudden minor pain in my right elbow. So-called "mouse and computer" pains. Why now? I haven't had those pains for weeks to months. Perhaps old man pain has jumped ship. The light of awareness chased his darkness from my shoulders. He had no place to go; so he's hiding, once again, in my right elbow.

I just chased old man pain into a corner.

But he never gives up. Still, if I can keep him on the run by constantly focusing the light of awareness on his miserable behind, I'll stay ahead in the battle.

"Point of Transformation"

Here's a radical new approach: Instead of doing each exercise by the number I should do it to the point of transformation. In other words, over and over again without counting, focusing on the feeling the exercise creates in my body and watching my body and mind being transformed by the constant repetition of focus on the exercise.

Counting the Numbers is Very Earthbound.

Focusing on Soft Power flowing into your body parts (forget counting and numbers) catapults you into the high-voltage world of magnetic force and electromotive energy.

It moves you from quantitative to qualitative.

Artists as Revolutionaries

I always admired revolutionaries. Artists are revolutionaries.

"There are only two kinds of artists: revolutionaries and plagiarists"—Paul Gauguin

Doing headstand, scorpion, and even Tsamikos variations in public are similar to playing "Alhambra" and "Leyenda" in public. Both are good exercises in focus and concentration.

I need a new challenge, a new adventure. Could it be running the marathon? Since I've done it before, can it be new? Perhaps, like all other miracle schedule activities, the new is really a renew. Renewal, renaissance, and resurrection are the order of the day.

It means a commitment to training. This means I must run in the mornings, on weekdays, and even on the days I teach folk dancing (light on those days.) This means finishing before 9:00 a.m. This means starting around 8:00 a.m. This means getting up at 5:00 a.m.

Start a new running log book. Make daily comments in it.

Celebrating

I've recorded most of my 78, 45, and 33 rpm folk dance records and tapes. Some mop ups are still left.

Eventually, I will fine tune.

I'll finish this recording first stage by Sunday.

What will I do once I finish?

Celebrate!

How?

By shouting "Yahoo!", clicking my heels, and running down the street!

Pace

My pace for the last twenty-five years (and maybe most of my life) has been fast. I worshiped speed as macho, dynamic, and vital.

Maybe my pace for the rest of my life will be slow. The pace of maturity, deepening knowledge, and wisdom.

Audio Engineering

The field is audio engineering.

Morning lost is part of cosmic depression.

Naming the field of audio engineering, writing it down, centers me and points out a direction.

Audio engineering is larger than the computer field. It envelops sound and number.

In the beginning was the Word. It lives in Sound and expresses itself through Music.

Audio engineering may be close to my soul.

This is my computer study year. Through back alleys, it leads to my Audio Center. Number, Pythagoras, Audio Center, and the Mystery may all work together.

Revisiting the Land of Enthusiasm

Could my old nemesis, denial of enthusiasm, be the reason for this long down?

No running, no exercise, mucho aches, no energy, no nothing.

Could this long low following my computer (and guitar) accomplishments be all about the squashing of enthusiasm. . . again?

I keep looking for new directions, new teachers, new ideas, new studies, new, new, new. Is it an attempt to avoid excitement over my accomplishments?

Accomplishments put me "there." I have arrived.

Where have I arrived? Where is "there?"

It is the land of enthusiasm, home of the simcha heart. I stand on top of the mountain laughing for joy, tossing hallelujahs into the sky and dropping huge "Wahoos!" into the valley below.

Have I been unable or unwilling to live in the intense heat of enthusiasm? Could be.

Time to rekindle, rethink, and revisit the heated heartland.

Only the Dead Go to Heaven

Florida makes me think about retirement. . .and death. Because to me, retirement is death!

I see my wife dying; I will lose her. I see myself dying, I will lose me. I see the world and all things I do in it as transience, and in the long run, meaningless. Yes, Florida illuminates and intensifies the retirement-equals-death equation.

Indeed, this is a very depressing symbolic aspect of Florida. People retiring, giving up their purpose, function, and life's work in order to play golf, tennis, and lie in the sun. Ugh, ugh, ugh!

Enclosed, fenced in, and guarded retirement communities, retirement prisons specializing in filling up time with fun activities, which, since they never affect society, are ultimately meaningless and empty.

Florida as nursing home for the soon-to-be-deceased.

Yes, some people see Florida as heaven on earth. I agree. But only the dead go to heaven.

Florida Folk Dance Camp was full of life.

Florida retirement communities are full of death.

Which shall I choose? Is there a compromise between life and death? Can one chose both?

Death will come to the body. This is natural. But perhaps retirement is worse than death! It is a living death. You feel all the pangs of the coffin as you are buried alive behind the walls of your "retirement community."

Kabbalah Fever!

Plus the "sales heat" from the Saturday night party in Lake Hiawatha with Sasha, the Tamburitzan performance Sunday, and tonight's Roma concert. All the sales and meeting excitement generated more and much fever. This, added to "Leyenda" and "Alhambra" fever, simply raise the heat quatient.

Breakthrough fun. It could be Kabbalah fever!

Watch out: Danger from an overabundance of sparks. They can break and burn my vessel.

Wallow

Enjoy the fruits.
Luxuriate in "alhambra" and CD success
Like a hippo, do nothing but wallow in the water.
Perhaps another mountain will appear. . . perhaps not.

Hit the bottom of the creative cycle yesterday. Dark artistic or cosmic depression. But in the pit of hell, I found new roots, and shot up through the stratosphere is a blast of historic rebirth!

Here's how I arrive at today's place:

First I wrote down some ideas: Slavic studies, Rabbinic studies (become or study to become a rabbi), Jewish studies, Computer studies.

Then I wrote: Become an expert in Eastern European culture: Byzantine, Jewish, Balkan, Slavic studies. A twenty-year project. Language and history.

Write a history of the Balkans, Hungary, Slavic, etc. My own history of and for tours, etc. A pamphlet or short history book. A Mad Shoe History Series.

What would happen if I "took off" on history? A Hungarian History book, Bulgarian, etc.

Combine language (one year) with history of the country, a tour, a write a Mad Shoe History of the country. Study the language, country history, then write my own Mad Shoe History of said country.

The Hero

I want to do something heroic with my life.

What is heroic? Working, sacrificing for a higher cause.

I cannot see the stock market as heroic or a higher cause. Fun when up, frightening when down, the money I make (and lose) there is ever a means to an end.

What is heroic to me?

Struggling to stay alive as an artist is heroic. Building JGI is heroic. Promoting and marketing my artistic creations, guitar, singing, folk dancing, writing, and study through world travel by building JGI is heroic.

Getting my soul out there to serve the public, standing up for my art is my form of heroism. Sure it's a business. But it is also heroic.

In fact, being in business, fighting to stay in business especially your own business, is heroic.

Most people discourage heroism. It's stupid, not sophisticated, and often frightening, they say. Why take a chance? Make it easy on yourself. Take the easy way out. Why stand above the crowd? You'll only get shot down. Plus your attempts to stand out may fail. You'll feel bad.

Well, I feel great when I'm a hero, especially my own hero. I can pound my chest with pride because I dared! I grabbed the horns, bucked the trend, pounded the gate, fought the fight, struggled, gave it my all.

Fighting for worth makes me worthy. Was I on the right path of life? Did I fight the good fight? Or did I waste my life dwelling among lesser things, afraid to make the effort, turning aside from my courage to grab the golden ring? Not everybody dares to be a hero. Not everyone wants to be a hero. But I do.

Talking to Others as Entertainment

Walking down the street and talking to strangers, or just about anyone, is a great source of entertainment.

In general, talking to people is social entertainment.

When I travel, I walk down the street, stop strangers, store keepers, whoever and wherever; and ask them whatever questions come to mind. I want to start them talking and see what happens. This adventure, speaking to others, to just about anyone, is a great source of travel stimulation.

Fixing Things as a Way of Life?

The spruce top of my Rubio guitar is separating from its body. It has to be reglued. This has never happened before! Now I must fix it, have it fixed. That means bringing it to Jim at DeBella's Music. Can I trust him with this valuable guitar? Isn't it time to insure it?

No question all things fall apart. . . and keep falling apart. They must then be fixed. It is a fact of life.

Can fixing things, putting things in order, be called a way of life? Can the spark of infinity be found in organizing and reorganizing things?

I must also buy a dehumidifier for the basement. I'll go to Sears. More fixing. Refixing the basement problem.

I have to insure my guitar and take care of our will. More fixing.

What does this have to do with tours, organizing events, creating, selling them, and making a living? Can a unifying spark of divinity be found in both? I'm sure it can. But it's up to me to find it.

It is I who have put the meaninglessness into "fix it." It is only I who can give it meaning.

Ultimately, there are two kinds of people: enthusiasts and squashers. The latter, nay saying, doubting "realists" are subtly dangerous. They murder dreams, kill joys, discount miracles, and doubt the glory of heaven.

As the Messiah said while washing his feet in the Jordan, "A little messianism never hurts."

On Leaders and Leadership

Much of the Byzantine history I read is about politics, kings, and emperors. Why would I be interested in them? How does reading and study of such histories affect me?

I am asking an important question: How do people lead? What qualities must they possess? Their position of authority creates many challenges for them. Since I am a leader, "How can I become a better one?" That is why I study history.

How does religion and mysticism play into leadership? What is the relationship between the leader, his (or her: witness the Byzantine Empress Irene) leadership, and God, the ultimate Leader?

I also want to lead on a worldly plane, to create an organization in material reality that is made out of people.

What is the relationship of creating to leading?

Why do people need leaders? It improves their focus.

Can a concert performer be called a leader? When I give a concert, am I a leader? Yes.

When I teach folk dancing, or anything else, can it be called leadership? Is a teacher a leader? Yes.

Leadership has many forms. Political leadership is but one of them. Yet it is important that I read about it and the diplomatic skills it entails.

Speaking Out on Political Subjects

Should I speak out on political subjects? Would that be a good direction for me? Would it help me understand, concretize, elucidate, and solidify my beliefs? Is it any use at all?

Can I, should I, use what I think to help explain myself to myself and others, and to help the world?

Would it help the world? Would it turn others against me? Probably. But I don't mind that. The real question is: would I even get through? Political discussions are really like frontal attacks. And such attacks often create equal and opposite reactions. The result is frustration and deadlock.

Art and folk dance teaching, however, create immediate agreement. How can you dance the hora in the same direction and disagree?

Thus art is an indirect means of creating agreement and oneness. And I like oneness.

Politics is about power. Its arguments often create divisions. It is often intellect fighting intellect. And the intellect is a very shallow surface.

Art goes straight to the bottom line substrate, the emotions.

Thus I ask again: Should I bother speaking out on political subjects? Will it end up to be only to hear myself talk to a blank and empty wall? Sure people will listen. But will they hear? And ultimately, will they change their beliefs because of me? Fundamentally, I doubt it.

But, on the other hand, maybe they will. . . even though such a change may take years.

Since I doubt such speech would be effective, that is, would change others, then the only reason I should approach and do it would be to effect and help change myself!

It might be good for me to speak publically about my views. I might learn not to feel so tongue-tied whenever a political subject. . . or even a historical, philosophical, or any other"serious: subject comes up. Notice how many subjects I added to "political." There are many subjects I feel completely to quite tongue-tied about. Again, these subjects, especially history and even philosophy, are ones I have been reading about and studying for years. I have lots of knowledge and even views there. But it is hardly ever verbalized.

So maybe it would be good for me to talk about my politics. And, in so doing, I might be able to buttress my arguments by references to history, philosophy, economic theory, etc. Again, I have a lot of non-verbalized knowledge in these areas.

There is a whole sleeping continent beneath my smiling face that is rarely unearthed or exposed. It lies there supporting my surface, but few know why this surface stays up. I know why. But I find it so difficult to verbalize or explain it.

I wonder why.

Probably it has to do with my background, my upbringing, even a feeling of being stupid politically. Perhaps it goes back to my bad marks in high school and college. I don't quite know what it goes back to, but it goes back to something. But maybe I will never find or know its origin. And maybe it doesn't even matter what the origin is. Maybe it is again only a question of being ready.

I may be ready for this next stage, the political explanation stage, the opening of history and the pouring of historical development knowledge into my writings and public discussions.

What would be a good bottom-line reason to do all this? It would help to better to know myself.

Computer Expert

Most of my day is now spent on the computer. Therefore, out of necessity, it is necessary for me to become a computer expert. This is a welcome shift in my attitude towards computers! It is can-do, will-learn coalescing of the new road that began last November when I studied the Nero CD creation program. David said I was good at computers. This threw the first sliver of light across the darkness of an old lack-of-computer-confidence self. The possibility of a new view of my computer self opened.

Nine months later (perfect gestation time), this view metamorphosized into computer expert.

Slavery "Lite"

Moving from the prison of purpose to lost in the wilderness land of free choice.

The chaos of this wilderness freedom is terrifying. The slavery prison of purpose is, although rigid, straight, and narrow, secure and safe. It focuses energies. When lost in the wilderness, disparate energies go in all directions. They search for focusing purpose.

I like my slavery. But I like it "lite."

The Great Practice of Self-Denial

How could I begin a life of self-denial?

This first thing I could denying myself is the luxury of discouragement. I could deny myself the "pleasure" of its delicious down feeling.

This asks another question: How to be ever optimistic? How to face this attitude challenge?

First step is the self-denial of discouragement.

This is a firm belief in progress. And this in spite of wars, conflicts, problems, and endless difficulties which can create clouds of pessimism. Clouds, indeed. But behind each cloud is the sun.

Pessimism sees transient clouds.

Optimism recognizes the eternal presence of the sun.

Practically, this means my arpeggio can still improve. . . and it just did! How? Through the new, dynamic, and different right hand relaxation in the root of the fingers!

Other things could improve too.

Optimism means an on-going belief in progress and improvement. Self-improvement and world improvement never end.

If I think this way, others might accuse me of naivety or being a pollyanna. Well. . . too bad! Deep down, it is the way I think. I just have to face it and believe in it. Believe in my own belief. Not a bad thing to do.

Computer Art and/or Multi-Media Artist

I can't do any more in my computer life. But at least I have established a direction!

It is contained in the words (title or rubric): Computer Art and Multi-Media Artist. Such a field includes Writing/Painting/Music or Language/Picture/Sound.

The idea crystallized when I looked at the artist's creations in my new Photoshop 7 book by Elaine Weinmann and Peter Lourekas. "Did you actually draw/paint these pictures on a computer?," I asked. "Using a mouse?" If yes, wow! I should learn it!

The new direction has all to do with computers—learn as much as I can about them, and the arts as expressed through use of computer and computer program skills.

These skills involve the knowledge of:

1. Dreamweaver: specialize in web design.

2. Quark: in writing and publishing skills

3. Nero: specialize in CD and music file creation skills, cover designs etc.

4. Photoshop: specialize in computer art and design skills.

5. Building a PC for Dummies: This plus other electronics, technical. and theoretical books specializing in the technical analysis, understanding, and knowledge of how computers are put together, how they work.

I may eventually even learn a computer language. Like HTML. A programming language. To know how programming works.

Micro-Running

John Dolan wrote me an E-mail:

"Thanks for the micro-running vibrations. I need them. Is the remark about 'great laughs in inner truths and great truths in inner laughs' yours? I like it."

I wrote him back:

"If, due to lack of courage and fear of public humiliation, you do not feel ready for outside micro-running, you can always do the inner version: Meditate on it real hard and slow."

Enthusiasm Reborn

After a year in the transitional wilderness, it is so nice to be enthusiastic, about something again.

Enthusiastic about computers! It could also flood backwards, reinvigorate, inspire, fuel, revivify, and bring new life into all aspects of the miracle schedule.

Computer study may (will) water the stationary, stagnant, limbo transitional old plants of guitar playing, singing, yoga, running, and even writing. It may create new and future flowers. Let the petals fall where they may!

Is that what this *New Leaf* is about? Are computers and computer study what lies Beyond Passion?

Perhaps Beyond Passion is not the right expression, the right combination of words. Rather, it may indicate a new kind of passion, a passion Beyond Passion, one kindled by science, organization, and numbers.

I am moving into the future by returning to the past. This new passion may tie into my high school romantic fascination with physics.

Problems are Forever

So much of computers is dealing with problems. Problems and problem solving.

Tour problems, money problems, relationship problems, business problems, artistic problems, organizational problems, sales problems, cosmic problems, all problems. Problems are forever. Computers point that out, highlight it: Problems appear suddenly, instanteously, and in most frustrating manner.

I need a positive and welcoming approach to daily problems. Will it help my attitude towards them? We'll see.

In fact, most if not all of life is problems and problem solving. Life is a problem; life is problem solving. Always has been, always will be.

Admit it, deal with it, love it, and move on. To what? The next problem, . . .and then. . . more problems.

Endorphin Release Program: Give It My All!

When I teach folk dancing halfway, holding back, not giving it my all, I get injured. I prevent healing endorphins from doing their work.

To release healing endorphins, give it my all.

I injured my hip a few weeks ago. Was it caused by overuse through running? Who knows? But after a few days of rest, the pain of the injury should have gone away. It didn't. And it still hasn't. So, like a John Sarnoian, I must ask why. Have I a vested interest in "keeping" the injury? After all, it could diverting my mind from up-coming tour fears.

Try the give-it-my-all approach. Its release of endorphins will heal me.

Basically, this morning I want to complain. I can't wait for our tour to end. I can't wait to go home, and get back to my normal physical existence with its running, calliyoga, and folk dancing.

Even though I like my tourists and the tour is going very well, nevertheless, I have had enough. I can't wait to get back to my life.

And yet, for now, this tour is my life. There are still about five days left. How will I survive them? What can I do to smooth the path until that beautiful times comes when this fucking tour ends?

And notice the "fucking." I'm trying to get mad at this tour. . . but I can't. I'm even trying to find some of my tourists to hate, to get mad at, or at least, get annoyed with. . . but I can't. None of the old self-energizing techniques seem to work anymore.

Yet, my left "tourist knee" is still semi-crippling me. And a good part of me refuses to dance, exercise, run, or even move fast until my responsibilities with this tour are over.

Strange, indeed. I feel I am killing my body for this tour. I am my own tour martyr. Why am I doing this? Why can't I take care of myself and my tourists? I don't know.

I have fixed and fixated my total focus and concentration on this tour, on running it well, on making sure every aspect is right and on doing everything I can to satisfy the desires and demands of each one of my tourists. Of course, their happiness is beyond my control; deciding to be happy is up to them. Yet I am doing everything in my power to fulfill my side of the bargain.

My mind (and body) is totally committed to running the best tour possible. This was one of the original promises and goals I gave to myself at the beginning of the tour. The other goal and promise was to run it *b'simcha*, with joy and love of God in mind. That mental leap, the creation and implementation of that attitude, I have not fulfilled. "Proof" is in the existence of my "tour knee" and the fact I have done no physical exercise, no yoga, running, calliyoga, no nothing, almost from day one of this tour.

My mind is out of my body, and my body in all its glory has been left behind.

Again I ask: What, if anything, can or should I do about this? What can I do to complete the *b'simcha* commandment? What can I do to make it part of my tour life?

How about the idea that I'm doing it already but do not know it? I am in the new process or merging *b'simcha*, tourism, and personal self-fulfilment (so far, without exercise), but I am not yet aware of it?

This is based on the question: Why would God punish me for running a tour? It is, after all, a mitzvah. A mitzvah tour. The only reason running such a tour could be seen as a "punishment" is because I have yet to see light in it. I have yet to merge its disparate elements into the unity and oneness that is the experience of Him.

Am I in the process of creating a new, post-transformational, resurrectional, renaissance tour form, one in which I can comfortably combine excellent organization, focus and concentration on itinerary, program and tourists, and satisfy my personal needs as well? In other words, is it possible to work and play at the same time?

Simultaneous work and play: Work becomes play, play becomes work. An ideal state. Could I do and think such a thing?

Although creating such a state of mind is difficult, it not impossible. Why not do it anyway?

How would I begin?

The first step would be reclaiming my body. I used to do that through running and calliyoga. But, so far, on this tour, I am not able to do them.

What are my choices?

1. Force myself to return to exercises. (This approach never works.)

2. Give up on the exercises at least for now. See where giving up leads me. It's an experiment. Can I survive without them? Will I become completely debilitated and out of shape? Or will this "forced exercise rest" actually improve my exercises when I return to the states? Gestation often works wonders. A nice thought. Perhaps it is the right thought.

Obviously, for some reason, I can do little to no exercises on tour. Maybe I am meant to take a personal exercise "vacation." Maybe it will be good for me. This is an optimistic approach. Some new attitude or approach may be cooking, marinating, but I don't know what it is.

I hope I am right. But hoping has its own truth. Hope may not make it so, but it is often a signal that seeds have been planted and future growth, in hitherto unknown directions, is up ahead.

Tour Self-Transition

I wanted to transform myself on this tour. The old tour self lived twenty years. After I completed last summer's Scandinavian tour, I felt I've done it all. The old tour self was no longer needed; it had served its purpose. Thus it died.

I was left without a tour self.

Last year came the period of transition.

Now I am in the rebirth, reconstruction phase, a renaissance mode. This is true in other parts of my life.

But evidently, I had to experience a new tour in order to understand and create a new self. I had to lead another tour to put the new tour self into play. As my pre-travel goal stated, the new tour self wanted to organize and run the best tour possible and do it *b'simcha*.

Exercise on tour, along with study, may have represented part of the old tour self, which, through withdrawal, stayed in touch with the old neighborhood self.

But the present post-transformational self, no longer needs to hide its enthusiasm from others.

It can, not only feel and express *b'simcha* in private, but it can express this quality in public. In so doing, it transfers positive vibrations to others.

I Love to Lead!

I am solidifying my post-tour leadership attitude.

I love to lead, especially when I can maintain my focus, concentration, and *b'simcha*.

Practice
You think total and concentration is easy?
Try it.
If you last ten seconds that's pretty good.
Keep practicing
The world of illusion is transient.
But practicing is forever.

Backaches, Travel, and Terror

We arrived in Halifax, Nova Scotia, last night. Nice Radisson suite we're staying in. Luxurious and big. Did rather full yoga last night to recover from the flight. A good thing.

Yet this morning my back hurts. Could it be from the yoga? Somehow, I doubt it. I'd rather think it is because: (a) I didn't bring my guitar and can't play this morning, (b) We're in a new place, a new environment, and I still don't have my bearings. I'm somewhat lost and disoriented and so my back hurts.

I like this psychological explanation much better than the usual arthritis one. It puts me more mental control; it also show how creative is my mind. . . that it should invent these protections for me, putting pain in my body to divert attention from my mind which actually hurts more, and is powerfully threatened by disorientation and the cosmic lost feeling.

Yes, although the pain in my back and body is limited, the pain in my mind is eternal, infinite, indeed cosmic. It threatens total destruction of body, mind, and spirit. Certainly, such a threat is infinitely worse than a mere back pain. How dare I consider it, even look at it! Well, my creative mind refuses too, and gives me a minimal, handleable back ache instead.

Is it really true? Could such disorientation really be such a threat to me, forcing me to cower, tremble, and run down my spine into my lower back? Can my psyche really be so threatened by such minor dislocations, by merely traveling somewhere else? Is leaving home really such a terror?

Evidently it is. But I don't dare look at it. Imagine that, here I am in the travel business, and travel itself scares the hell out of me. (Maybe that's why I'm in it: to understand and even conquer my fear.)

The excitement, adventure, and thrill of travel is obvious. Everyone talks about it, praises the exploration of new places, lauds the daring and adventure of it. There is also the lure of a hidden and possible paradise in some distant and yet undiscovered place.

But I've been to many countries and still haven't found paradise. Oh yes, I've found adventure, problems, joys, sufferings, sorrows, and beauties. But peace of mind? Not exactly.

Am I looking for peace of mind?

Not exactly.

But I am looking for joy. No question that back aches, terror seizures of leaving home, the anxiety of travel, certainly diminish any hopes of such lofty emotions.

Is there anything I can do about all this?

Is there any way to incorporate the *b'simcha* attitude into travel? Or must I stay home and play guitar in order to do it?

Maybe I will never lose this uncomfortable disorientation or conquer this fear. Should I give up travel? I've reached a *b'simcha* point in guitar playing; maybe it is time for me to play my guitar. . . all day long!

Temper Tantrum

To travel, you have to be flexible. But who's flexible? I want to have things my own way.

Part of me is definitely enjoying this tour. Notice I say tour, not vacation. Well, for me, that may be progress. I've already decided that so-called "vacations" are not good for me. I need work, structure, direction; I need something to focus on in order to stay sane and healthy. Falling into the vacuum of vacation, into the abyss of nothingness, only annoys, nay, terrifies me. Forget it.

So, see this trip to Nova Scotia as a tour, for me, may well be progress.

That means there is something in it for me. This attitude itself is a radical departure and admission.

If I like it, then I will have to take complete responsibility for my pains; I'll have to admit I'm creating them for my own reasons. I can no longer blame this trip on trying to please my other. Oh, of course, that's part of it. . . but only part. By recognizing that there is definitely something in this trip for me, opens me up to an entirely new way of thinking. Although I am overburdened, even overwhelmed by tours and touring, nevertheless, pushing myself (even through pleasing another), may be good for me.

It is the pushing myself concept.

Indeed, I am pushing myself to come to Nova Scotia. But I am also resisting while I push. Thus I am somewhat stuck in the center with my brakes on. Is this push-pull, forward-resist causing a type of mental paralysis which is being expressed in my frozen muscles, stiff and painful back, sharp periodic stabbing pains in the knees, and shoulders, and who knows where else?

Am I having a temper tantrum because I can't go forward or backwards. I'm stuck in the mud of attitudinal indecision.

Well, no question I am having a temper tantrum. I am just not sure yet of its cause.

If I admit I am benefitting from and even enjoy this tour, then I might even have to give up my (delicious) anger. It might even change the fundamental structure of this relationship. I have grown so in opposition. Can I afford to give it up? What will happen to me? Is this the real and fundamental threat to my former attitude, world view, and even existence?

I would have to exchange anger for love and appreciation. Could I even exist in such a vacuum? Where would the bite, the spice, the pepper, paprikas, and even the salt come form?

And am I even right in this very fundamental analysis?

I'd have to give up my back pain. . . for love?

Give up back pain? Never!

The Poetry of Calliyoga

Arm rotations: developing wings, starting to fly.

Side pushes: pushing away the evil, negative forces.

Wrist rotations?

Neck rotations: Neck as gateway. Unscrewing the lid. Loosening. . . and opening the trunk. Letting positive, celestial vibrations pass through the head to enter and fill the entire body.

Lateral bends: Kidneys as waterway. Loose and loosening the lower back, watery entrance to the bottom.

Right leg side extension: Opening the sexy bottom power.

Left leg side extension: More of the same.

Heel taps: Minor thigh work. Posture focus.

Heel lifts: The calves awaken. Posture focus.

Achilles heel stretch?

Right leg forward extension: ham string macerators. Lower back focus and function. Swimming river down the ham string leg.

Left leg forward extension?

Both: very technical. Emotions to the ham string are cut off. What is the emotion locked in a ham string? What is its feeling? What is a ham string? What are the religious, spiritual, metaphysical, and celestial aspects of a ham string. . . and of the plural, ham strings?

Right leg semi-squat dips and bounces: Quadriceps, hello. Quadriceps: power and strength personified! Wide open and sunny.

Left leg semi-squat dips and bounces: Power and strength personified on the dark, slippery, sinister side. The underworld opens its hoary and ancient gates.

(Knees: Where do knees fit in?)

Salute to the Sun: I've invented and developed micro-running, and it works.

How about inventing and developing micro-yoga?

Tour Leader of Life

I've decided to be a tour leader on my vacation. That means I've given up on vacations. It means I shall never take a vacation.

And why should I ever want to take a vacation? What will I take a vacation from? I've organized my life so I can be on vacation every day. Vacation, in this sense, means following my passion, passions, and dreams on a daily basis.

Thus I never want to take a vacation in the traditional sense of the word. It would mean taking a vacation from what I love doing. Paradoxically, such a vacation would mean for me means doing what I do not like, not following my passions, not following the path of my dreams, not fulfilling the beautiful daily requirements of my miracle schedule.

Why would I even consider taking a vacation from the vacation I am already on? Ridiculous.

Yet old concepts of vacation die hard.

My old one died on this Nova Scotia trip.

I have entered another Scotia, a Nova Terra Firma, Nova Via. I am now a tour leader of life.

This is a very good thing.

How does one maintain *b'simcha* joy under the public gaze of a lunatic, an incensed patron of the arts, an enraged traveler, an unhappy tourist, an angry customer, or blaming wife?

First, check out if you have personally done anything wrong. Is there anything you can fix, improve on, or change for the better? Although you may not have directly caused or be responsible for the happiness or unhappiness of others, maybe there is nevertheless, something you can do personally to improve the situation.

Once you have checked this out, and see there is nothing more you can do, first protect your physical self from damage. Then return to the *b'simcha* point.

New York Times versus the *Wall Street Journal* and *New York Post*: On describing reality as it is: Using the word "terrorist" versus all the verbal dishonesties and disguises such as "militant," "fighters," "kidnappers," and "insurgents."

It makes me furious. So narrow-minded, pig-headed, politically correct, and cowardly. What can I do about it? Basically, nothing. If people want, desire, plea to be fools, so be it. Perhaps my only questions should be: 1. Why does it bother me? 2. Why do I waste any time at all thinking about them?

These are questions I have control over; I do control my own mind. . . mostly. But as to how they think, how they remain so totally stupid, I have no control over. They are free to be the idiots that they are.

But again, why do I waste my mental energies on them?

I get so frustrated when they won't see it the right way. . . my way! But they don't, and they won't. I can't change their views one iota. Truly, it makes me want to scream. And I do. Still, nothing happens. Fury and frustration remain.

Perhaps all I can do is write about it.

Writing about it relieves some frustration, vents some anger, and is, evidently, my only. . .and perhaps best. . .form of self-empowerment.

Sputter and fume. Maybe writing about politics is the way to go. A creative and righteous approach to stupidity, injustice, and rage.

Take My Stand

I have been running, running away from myself, my talents, my excellence, goodness, skills, virtues, and more. I've run as much as far as I can, as far as I want to go.

I'm sick of running.

I'm taking my stand, here and now. . . for excellence!

How?

I miss my creative self. I mourn its demise.

Has it gone away at all, or is it in hiding?

The Campaign

An experiment: Put aside guitar bookings, and concerts for a year. Let guitar, bookings, singing become a "hobby." They will remain just as psychologically and physically important as writing, yoga, and running. But they will not be the center of my business focus. They haven't been for years, anyway.

This year's main project will be: How to run a sales campaign, how to promote and sell all my tours.

There is a certain sadness in this realization: I am, in a sense, giving up my inner world's of imagination and "creativity" on order to pursue function and connection in the outer world. It feels like I am betraying my fertile old world of imagination and in-room quirky but sustaining power, turning it in, to pursue outer connection with others.

Something is happening, but I don't quite know what it is. (That is why this journal writing is, and no doubt will always be, so personally important to me. Through it, I discover and explain myself to myself.)

Last year, I felt that, after twenty-five years of labor, I had finally fulfilled all my dreams. A success, indeed. But also, what a downer. I had to think about: What now? It threw me into a transitional year.

Then, on my tour to Slovenia, Croatia, and Hungary, I was reborn.

New tour realizations, ideas, and directions flowed in. I came back reinvigorated and inspired.

Upon returning, I spent all of September completing my tour itineraries, and basically, setting up my schedule and brain, and pointing it in a forward direction.

Thursday I finished that project. All my fliers are now printed. All information on my web site is up to date. All my dance classes have started, and I'm doing my first booking today. Thus I am now ready to begin my post-transitional year. I am ready to begin my campaign.

My heart and soul are going into this campaign. All my side efforts will be dedicated to this campaign.

I can't get used to seeing and believing how stupid and anti-democratic people on the left have now become. So many are my friends and colleagues. But their vision has so ossified, narrow, and biased. Deep in my habitual heart, I just cannot believe what I see before my eyes. Bigoted, intolerant, and anti-democratic? The wonderful, civil-rights believing Left? It goes against all my upbringing and former judgements. But it is nevertheless, true.

Beneath this, I am facing the question of believing that I have a political belief, of having confidence in my own vision of history.

I believe in individualism, the liberty of the entrepreneur, the freedom of the artist. These personal beliefs, which I have always had and am now developing even further, have slowly been translated into political beliefs, beliefs in political liberty, pursuit of individual excellence, and ultimately, democracy.

While my old world of the left drifts into ossification, anger, and intolerance (sometimes even bordering on fascism), I become stronger in my outward, gone-public, political beliefs of democratic individualism, liberty, and freedom.

These are political and social words that express the inner core of my beliefs, the essence of my artistic soul.

The artistic vision through my in-room world of fantasy and dream-idea experience; the political vision I am slowly developing is my outward, gone-public expression of this in-room vision.

Believers that Saddam Hussein could be contained by sanctions, that he would never get, have, or use WMD, that he would not pass them on to terrorists, that he was not a threat to the civilized world, and that he should not have been forcibly removed, are either stupid, naive, blind, or all three.

Entering the Political World

I am usually tongue-tied in the expression of my political view. This has been a life-long frustration. Words just don't come out easily. True, I live now mostly among the opposition, and my views may be dangerous for my job. Among the folk dance world, I may indeed lose customers if I express my views. But this danger is not what frustrates me. (I can recognize such a realistic, job-related danger; I can deal with the intolerance of my tolerance loving liberal friends.)

But no. I have a built-in, life long, type of aversion to expressing myself in politics. As soon as I open my mouth, my tongue starts moving backwards; I retreat into the center of my mind, and there I find a field full of mush. And this despite the fact that I am smart, know facts, and am well read in history. I am not going to analysis why I am so tongue-tied. But now am ready to Move past it.

Such a move will not help me economically. It's won't get me more bookings, jobs, or customers for my tours, weekends, and dance classes. But it will relieve me of deep and ongoing frustration. It may also help me deal with the intolerance that rises in my mind when I talk to the opposition. It is expressed in the sentence: "I can't believe how stupid these people are." Or "How can so-called educated people be so naive and dumb?"

Deep in my heart, I cannot understand why others cannot see things the way I do.

Are my thoughts and thought-process really so unique? Am I really that different? Why don't people see things the way I do? It is all so obvious to me.

Nevertheless, just because the sun rises, and shines in their eyes, does not mean people will see or believe it. Nothing I say or do will make them see it. The blind remain invested in their blindness. Nothing but a catastrophe or miracle will make them change. Even that might not work. I stand amazed at my powerlessness to change the mind of others.

Nevertheless, I might lessen my frustration, and even "accept" the folly of others, if I sink my mind into social readings and political works.

We'll see where this leads, or if indeed, it leads anywhere.

But at least for now, it is a reading direction.

Also I will tie my love of artistic freedom to the more abstract, political love of freedom.

I hate slavery, bureaucracy, and most often, the opinions of others when they don't agree with mine.

Does this express intolerance, a belief in myself, or combination of both? Good questions.

This may also be part of love of intellect which I discovered at the University of Rochester, Aix-en-Provence, and the University of Chicago. There I discovered books, reading, philosophy, and ideas. I loved reading about them, and the fact that such ethereal things existed. But my own inadequacies, plus the dozens of intellectual snobs around me, helped silence any verbal displays.

I didn't quite understand my own passion for learning. This love was based on the spiritual melt-down magnificence experienced during a Beethoven symphony. A mystical, non-verbal, spiritual, an oceanic merging with the universe. How could I explain such a thing to secular, non-religious, semi-communist friends, or even to myself who, at that time, believed in all that ideological nonsense.

Rebirth of Body and Mind

The body dies, and with it the mind.

On its ashes a new body and mind are resurrected.

One needs the Great Depression to clean out remnants of the old; this creates a vacuum, a "depression," into which the new will flow.

Strangely, part of last year's experiment was to see how little I could do with my body, I much I could hold back, minimize my exercise routines and see how long I could survive.

"Can I survive doing less?" was my question.

The answer was "yes," but without the stimulating, world-blowing, mind-boggling endorphin release of giving it my all, taking a chance of hurting myself by "doing too much," taking a chance of injury and pain in order to break boundaries. This was my strange experiment.

The experiment has run its course, and it was successful. The answer I came up with is: "no."

Due to fear of the spontaneous forces of a free society, unleashed largely by the French Revolution, the French utopians developed the governing ideas of socialism.

Is that why I never understood all these intellectual discussions by my socialist/communist friends, Mark Axelrod, the Socialist Club I belonged to, even that Russian history professor everyone admired, at the University of Chicago?

Perhaps deep in my heart, I was always the rebel, the individualist, the artist seeking my own personal vision. I sensed a deep danger in the authoritarian dictates of utopian socialism and communism but was, as yet, too self-ignorant to acknowledge or even consciously understand it.

But I sensed it. And in my instinctual self-preservation mode, I retreated. One of my retreat methods was to "not understand" it, to become "anti-intellectual," ever hating the snobbery and pomposity of such elites, and developing my own love of the common man which I express in folk dance classes by including every klutz and clod on the block.

I have a deep love of the klutz. I prize them well above the intellectual snobs, and pompous know-it-alls of my University of Chicago days. But I only recognize this forty years later.

So many intellectuals bought into the doctrines and philosophy of socialism and communism. They still do. They believed its specious promises of greater freedom from economic necessity. Why are they still such fools? This question has still not been answered.

Are most intellectuals cowards who have retreated into their intellect for protection?

Do they suffer from a deep-seated inferiority complex which they have yet to face? Did this start in childhood, during school days or earlier, when they were threatened or beaten up by the tough local kids in their neighborhood?

Were they taught not to fight or worse, that they couldn't fight?

Mourning: A Dying Week

Just as I am going backwards, to re-record old songs and records, review and write down old choreographies, and edit old New Leaves, so should I also be moving forward with and towards something new.

Just as old friends are dying, as I mourn the past and my past lives with them, so too look towards the future, the younger people behind me, and a life beyond death. The old dies, the new is born. . .and reborn. I mourn the passing of my old life and its attachments and old friends such as Batya, Eleni's husband David (whom I did not know), and my wonderful mime teacher, Tony Montanaro.

Death and passing. Sure it puts my mortality right up front. Eventually my family, friends, me, all of us, will be on our way.

It's a transient phase, though surly it makes everything I do seem worthless. It is the biggest "Why bother?" supporter I know. Why bother going on, why bother doing anything, when all of it, friends, family, attachments, will simply wither away and slowly, or quickly, die?

How to go past this deception? Go right into it. Live in the knots and drowning. Wait for the rowboat to appear. Then pick up the oars, put the heavy, new, sad burdens in the boat, and row on out.

But today I'm in the thick of the sad-hanging trees and mourning swamp.

Learning about the death of Tony Montanaro was the final blow in a dying week.

Cultural Shifts. . . Forty Years in the (Democratic) Desert

In the 1960s, expressing emotion became the litmus test for authenticity and authority. If you feel something deeply and express it, it must be true. Thus the emotion of hatred for Bush became in important (the most important, the only important) part of the Democratic Platform.

Also came admiration of childlike fears. "I'm frightened" became an accepted and admired (for the authenticity) political and otherwise emotion.

From this also came, no doubt, admiration (and even respect) for the victim and victimhood. "I'm a victim! My victimhood is important. You must pay attention, feel sympathy, and listen to me because my downtrodden state is based on an authentic emotion."

A cultural shift: Instead of being ashamed of feeling hatred, fear, fearful, of becoming a victim, and thus fighting against it with all your might, you drift into admiration of these miserable states. The advent and near worship of psychology, the growth of the psychology business, nay industry, helped create a gigantic cultural shift, a worship, respect, and admiration of business-increasing negative emotions. These helped increase patient attendance and fed the nascent, new and growing, psychology business. It started in the 1960's (but, I believe, had its roots in the communist party hatred of free enterprise, capitalism, and the capitalist class.)

Indeed, people are now proud of their fears, proud to express them. It makes them feel and appear more authentic. There is a whole industry based on opening up and exploring such fears, expressing childhood and childlike hatred, and other emotions. Usually, the only emotion missing is joy! How much money can you make with joy, anyway? Who'll go to a therapist to learn how to handle it?

Joy is out. Fear, misery, and negativity simply make more money.

The human psyche thrives in opposition. This is true in the individual psyche and collective mind expressed through politics. This cycle of opposition grew is now in the process of dying. It has taken about forty years. Moses and God knew something about the number forty and the forty year period. Old-way attitudes, and the generations that embody them must, evidently, die before you can move on to the next stage of development. Make way for the next generation.

Just because those around me are depressed about the election results is no reason for me to suppress my jubilation. Although, I don't have to rub it in and gloat, nevertheless, I have to admit, I do enjoy the arrogant, stunned political opposition in pain and disarray.

It is a sad, nostalgic time. I am reviewing my past. Two Sundays ago I listened to my old records. Yesterday, I dipped into the cupboard and pulled out a sheaf, nay envelopes, filled with old letters, complementary of ancient performances, folk dances, weekends, and other deeds.

It is hard to get my bearings. I've stopped reading and studying. But I'm playing guitar, and even starting to sing, again. Also, I'm returning to the past, daring to look at it again, daring to draw from it certain pieces to sew together in a new cloth tableau. I'm creating the a foundation, based on the past, so that I can eventually, once again, head into the future.

I'm not there yet. I'm dwelling in nostalgia. What is nostalgia? Why is a revisit of the past so sad? It points to the transience of human existence. And no doubt, before I can absorb and accept my past, I have to make some kind of peace with it, incorporate it into my being. In so doing, I'll slowly drop my attachment to its old forms. Then I can move on.

Perhaps the sadness of nostalgia comes from breaking old attachment bonds. New seeds cannot be planted or flourish while the garden is still filled with old plants and flowers.

Adding Some Physical Reality to my Journal

Shouldn't I give a few sentences of physical reality to my journal? For example, this writing is taking place at the Land of the Vikings Lodge in Sherman, Pennsylvania, where I am now running a Mad Shoe Weekend. The morning air is crisp and cold; a light snow covers the ground. I sit alone at a round table in the morning dining room, pen in hand, writing in my journal. I've just finished making delicious coffee in the LOV coffee maker. Tony Montanaro's book, Mime Spoken Here, lies in front of me. I imbibe of its magnificent pages.

This morning I am giving a "physical reality" to my guitar music by focusing on feeling the strings as I play: Feeling the string roll from my finger tip, across my nail, and then following the sound in produces on its expanding way through the universe.

The focus is mental, the feeling is physical, the resulting (visual and aural) expansion is spiritual.

Inner Madman

Normal is a boring state of mind.

We need madmen! They travel to Mars. They conquer space both inner and outer.

Where is my inner madman? Hiding and/or resting.

I need to find him again.

The madmen of history are my heros.

Any novel I write should be about such a madman. Otherwise, why bother.

Is Catskill Moses a madman? Partly.

Or would a historical subject like Columbus be better?

Could I combine both in one?

Catskill Moses as the Columbus of the Mind.

Or do I need an entirely new character?

The "Mature" Child

The child develops into an adult through the maturation process. Once this has been completed, the matured adult can return to childhood. . .but this time as a "mature" child.

Jump-Starting my Mental Engine

I am annoyed by computer problems, age, guitar playing problems, death, relationships, up-coming events, whatever. But I am not afraid or terrified.

Without the motivation of fear, nay terror, what will I do?

Last year I was motivated by the terror of Florida Folk Dance Camp. I had to learn Nero, make CDs, and write up the dances. It took me months to prepare; three months of computer lessons, one month to put all my folk dance records and tapes on file, make folder by nation of folk dances, and create a collection of folk dance CDs. It was a gigantic project motivated, in part, by the terror of public humiliation if I did not succeed.

So I succeeded.

The year before I studied web design. I was in a similar rush to learn to create my own web site, use the internet, and through these skills, increase my tour sales. That project also took over three months and colored my year. It too, was motivated by the same fear, laden with doses of terror, that I would not succeed. Frankly, the whole computer idea, working with computers, frightened and frustrated me. There were also significant dabs of terror when the whole thing seemed to fall apart. I was so dependent on my teachers.

This year I put together the Florida Folk Dance Camp materials in a week. Now I look ahead, and truly, I seem to only have a few hours more work until I am finished! Rather than fear, terror, and frustration, I am experiencing an ease bordering on boredom! This is an amazing accomplishment. But like every accomplishment, every victory, it is met with the down question of: "What now? Where will I go? What can I do now to motivate myself?" And perhaps beneath that question is the strange one: "Where can I find some fear, nay terror, which will jump-start my mental engine and drive it into action?"

These days I've got frustrations. But I have no bottom-line fears or terrors. Since I gave up the stock market and decided to make money only through my own earnings, even the fear of financial insecurity has dropped away. The terror is gone. Only annoyance sprinkled with frustration is left. Fear and terror no longer drive me.

The old lynch-pin energy producers have fallen away. Part of me misses my fear and terror. They often created great forward visions and long-term goals. Frustrations and annoyances seem to engender only minor visions and short-term goals.

One great fear was public humiliation. Through growing self-confidence, that has diminished.

The "Now what?" question keeps emerging.

I hate to be afraid. I hate to be terrorized. Yet, without these hated feelings, I fall into a dustbin of sluggishness, of listlessness. How strange is the human mind.

Should I seek out fear? Should I seek out something, a "higher goal," an unreachable star, a vision beyond my eyes? Should I begin a quest that will terrify me? Maybe.

Falling Asleep

I've always wondered what that "falling asleep" feeling is that I have when I play guitar, or that comes before performances.

It is me "sitting on my fear and terror," pushing it down, denying its importance and power, dreading its coming and appearance. The common term is "pre-performance anxiety." But it is much more than that. It is the dread of a cosmic power running through you, taking control, destroying your ego, and everything once theoretically important to you.

But I still want to jump-start the power of freshness, the *pow* of miraculous revelation.

Computer problems are annoying. Am I supposed to find my miracles within these annoyances? But what else can I do? Things and mental attitude are going so fucking well! I can't stand all this so-called success! And yet I can't get out of it either. I'm stuck in a good place. So ironical. I'm used to being down. Now I'm up! I miss the creative juices of downs, yet I can't find or turn them on.

I have to deal with this flattened state of success. It is, indeed, a mental state, an attitude, since the outside world still brings me tsuras as it always did. Only now I see, in every tsura it brings, a "been there, done that." There are minor variations to each new tsura, but nevertheless, the concept is so familiar to me.

I'm at a bland, middle of the road, quiet, calm state. It's vaguely peaceful as the waves of annoyance roll over me.

Completely New

If enough rain drops keep falling on a rock, after many years, one day, the rock will suddenly crack. Same with the rock of brain-created attitudes. Tiny raindrops of self-confidence keep falling on it, and, after many years, one day it suddenly cracks.

This crack took place about three months ago.

Some results are:

1. Everything I do feels easier.

2. Since it is easier, I no longer feel the fear, terror, gush of enthusiasm or excitement when I do something. Everything feels "all right," or medium. There is kind of a blasé "I've done this before; I've done it all before." How can a "mere" repeat, a repetition be as exciting, thrilling, or create the same fear/terror of failure as it used too. I "know" the final result even before I finish.

3. This self-confidence exists despite my aches and pains, rejections and loses. I see them all as annoyances, but they touch not my core of confidence. Somehow I'll get along. But if I don't, somehow that's okay too. Whatever I do, get along or not, the substratum of self-confidence (tempered by "I've done it all before") remains.

I do not believe my self-confidence will vanish. It has been a long time in coming. Somehow it is here to stay.

My former lack of confidence helped create surprise, terror, enthusiasm, and excitement.

I have to "go forward" by returning (going backwards) to the miracle schedule. As I say, there is no other choice for me.

I have received a whack of self-confidence. This blow has knocked me down, thrown me off balance. I stand stunned, speechless, in awe before it. I don't know what direction to take, how to handle it, what to do. So I stand there and do nothing. On the surface, this "feels" blasé, and colored by "I've done it all before." But deep down, I may just be in the many month process of recovering from this life attitude-shattering blow.

The way I see it, a confident self is exactly what my mother did not encourage. Although she would not have denied me this attitude, she would not encourage it either. She would have greeted it with the question: "Are you tired?"

Now I am creating the ultimate rebellion.

It has taken me just about a lifetime to reach this state. Now it is time to turn this state into a new country.

Sudden Fatigue and the Burden of Excitement

Suddenly, I feel fatigue.

It might be due to the suppression of my incipient excitement over finding the Chi Running Next Level.

Yes, my fatigue was due to the billowing up of the excitement factor. This is the first whiff, hint, chill of excitement I have felt for months!

Notice how the "sudden fatigue" induced by suppression of excitement took place in my left shoulder. Bearing, carrying the heavy burden of joy on my shoulders.

Its suppression is manifested, physically materialized, represented, and expressed through the resistence pain in my left shoulder.

Parenthetically, four days later, on the morning of December 29, my mother's birthday, I awoke with no shoulder pain.

The "I Love You" Headache

I have a headache this morning.

Could it be because I am full of love?

My son says he loves me. He says I am a wonderful father.

Such words they fill me with an overflow of conflicting emotions. I don't know what to do with them.

I am stunned by their overwhelming power. It is God coming to visit, facing me in His Awesome Flesh. I am awed by His sudden appearance, through my son, in the "I love you, Dad" form.

In my upbringing, such words were understood, but rarely if ever uttered. Such feelings were left unspoken.

Today, I don't know how to react to "I love you." I don't know how to "defend" myself against it.

Now there's a funny word: "Defend." I feel I must defend myself against "I love you."

Where does this come from? It has little to do with God. . . and much to do with mother.

When Ma said (or even implied) those magic "I love you" words they made me feel guilty. Then I would have to do anything she asked.

How did I then respond to her "I love you?" Run like hell! Get out of here real fast. Otherwise, I'd be overwhelmed. I'd have to give in to all her demands, lose my identity and personhood. I'd end up totally squashed.

This control device came straight from Mother. My father would never say or think such a thing.

If I remove my upbringing with its negative reaction to "I love you," what is left? The same satisfaction and fulfillment feeling that comes after a successful concert, weekend, tour, folk dance class, bar mitzvah, or other event, when an audience member comes up to me and says, "Great job!" or "I really enjoyed your program," or "Thank you!"

Personal satisfaction for a job well done equals "I love you." The job of fatherhood, husbandhood, familyhood, even a job of friend-shiphood: all jobs well done. Instead of thanking me by saying "Job well done," they say "I love you."

What is my response to an audience member when they compliment me? I say, "Thank you," or "I'm so glad you liked it."

What does David mean when he says "I love you?" Of course, on one level, I'll never know unless I ask him. But, on my own personal level, the way I see it, he is saying: "Dad, you did a good job bringing me up. Job well done!"

Can I see fatherhood as a "job?" Doesn't that make it crass, reduce its sanctity?

Yes and no. If job means alienated labor, yes. If job means (as in my own work) fulfillment and satisfaction through a total creative and loving effort, no.

An overflow of love. Was that the source of many of my former headaches. I thought most came from repressed anger. But maybe, on a deeper level, they came from repressed love. I created a dam between the Ocean of Love and my smaller ego/self: I pushed behind it to hold back the Ocean of Love. Pushing back this potential Flood created my headaches.

Well, I'm sick of these headaches. Time to let the waters in, deal with the waves, learn to ride and bob upon them.

Let the Ocean of Love flood my ancient Holland. Upon its waters, a new island will appear.

Chi Running Guitar

Chi Running has universal principles. How can it be applied to my guitar playing?

Loose hanging arms (fingers and wrists will follow).

Focus mind on Chi body center (in T'ai Chi and Chinese language: dan tien) located just below the navel and in front of spine.

Good mind practice. I also like using the word or name dan tien. It gives me an introductory intimacy with the Chinese language.

As I play guitar, I'm watching my mind move from my body center, dan tien (a new guitar playing experience) to my shoulder, then wrist and fingers. When I do, I see tension in the latter areas.

Also as I move my stomach muscles around the dan tien, I have a "familiarity." I remember being here before. . .but without recognition.

Leg Viewing

Now I'm trying Chi running techniques with my Dance/Yoga exercises. My legs feel so relaxed and light. Appendages to my body center. It feels so easy.

Lifting, stretching, pushing my legs. If feels like I'm hardly working at all.

A completely new way of looking at my legs.

Taking the Chi Challenge

I'm taking the Chi Challenge. What is it?

The Chi Challenge asks: How far and deep can I relax? In all my activities, how far and deep into relaxation can I go. . . in all things? How much energy (Chi) can I touch when I play guitar, run, perform yoga asanas, dance exercises, and follow my miracle schedule routines with Chi Challenge in mind.

It is a Universal Philosophy and Approach, applicable in all things.

I've known about Chi for years; I've known about its challenges. But the challenge is to now apply it, do it, make it a daily part of my life. Not even part of my life: The center of my life!

Daily, even hourly, practice is the only way to begin.

Let's try it daily for three months. See what happens.

On Blaming the Victim

Twenty years ago people would blame the victim.

Today is has fallen out of style. Victims have become blameless.

But blaming the victim is coming back. We are slowly and partially returning to the old form: And this is a good thing.

Why?

First, by assuming some responsibility for their situation, victims validate their own power! By accepting the idea it is (partly) their own fault, victims no longer have to wait for fate or others to step in. They can think and take action for themselves. "I can do something; I can help myself." This is good thing.

Often, the best self-defense is blaming yourself. Then, instead of looking outward for aid, you can start taking some self-help action.

As a by product, you help others.

Dare to Heal!

I talked to Deena about her Klezmer CD. I had lots to ask and say to her.

Perhaps one of my jobs is to motivate and inspire the next generation. David said I should become a healer. I understood what he was talking about even though I don't relate to healers. Yet I know what healing is.

Inspiring, motivating others is my form of healing.

Eleni's husband died. I visited her a few times, talked to her. She liked many of the things I said. Perhaps the above applies to Eleni as well.

I'm also thinking about Dottie's arthritic neck problem. Is there anything I could do about it? If I can heal my knee, make its sudden pain go away, through internal Chi relaxation technique, could I do the same for Dottie?

Dare to heal!

Dare to heal myself. . . and others. Make that my next mantra.

Mmy folk dance teaching heals others. It is an indirect approach.

Vibrations of folk dancing cure as do those of guitar playing. I know I can heal. But it has always come as a by-product of art. An accident, even a footnote. I do not feel "responsible" for the healing results. And yet, I am.

Truth is, I am hesitant to take responsibility. I believe that God cures. I do my thing, then get out of the way. In the process, the higher forces step in, take over, and, in their mystical and powerful way, heal.

These higher powers work with and through me. I am their pawn.

Although the higher forces released through art are ultimately responsible, nevertheless, there is no question that part of me is responsible, too.

I am partly responsible for healing. That's a start.

If I could directly heal, what would that mean? Isn't it hubris-filled and arrogant? Would I not worry that I am fooling myself, becoming messianic, getting really crazy, moving beyond the pale of humanhood? I worry about letting myself slip into arrogance, breaking the second commandment, and, worshiping myself as an idol instead of God Himself?

And yet, I would be doing good by trying to heal others.

Of course, ultimately, only the healed can decide if he or she is healed. This decision is arrived at independently and has nothing to do with the healer.

Isn't this problem similar to my problem of sales. I am afraid I will force my product down someone else's throat, force my will upon them, and they will have no choice but to succumb. . .and buy something they really don't want. I hear the voice of my mother and all the communists ringing in my ears. Dirty capitalist pigs! Crooked salesmen! Lying thieves! These words are not a good healing start.

So, just as I have learned to mistrust my sales power, so I may have learned to mistrust my healing power. After all, what is healing but simply making someone feel good.

Making someone feel good is not so complicated. Perhaps healing, like folk dancing, is really not that complicated. And since I know how to teach folk dancing directly, I may well know how to heal directly.

When I teach folk dancing or perform any other public activity, I start off in disrepair. It is my task to heal myself. In the process of healing myself, I heal others.

Our collective task to heal ourselves. This can be facilitated by a group leader.

Forty Years in the Desert

Maybe Greeks need less time than Jews. Odysseus was away for twenty years. Moses was away for forty.

Maybe Jews needs forty years wandering in the desert before they can find themselves and return home.

Adrienne

I was also too quick in telling Adrienne about leading the line backwards. It made her nervous. After all, it was her first time leading. She was probably self-conscious to begin with. I should have watched and waited. I jumped too fast.

Non-Artistic Life

When my mind is scattered, jumping, and overwhelmed by contradictory thoughts—so many things I must do—this is a perfect example of how not to focus.

However, there is another way of looking at it: If I see the jumping itself as part of the art of flexibility, a focused flexibility. Then I can easily jump from one thing to another.

The Overwhelmed Feeling: Focusing the Mind

Part of me wants to be overwhelmed. Even though I hate it, I must like it, too.

Why?

First, overwhelmed give me a sudden purpose, function, and focus. My focus is to immediately or as quickly as possible free myself from being overwhelmed.

I jump from scattered mind to focused mind, from monkey mind to Chi mind. This aspect of overwhelmed is good.

The bad part of overwhelmed is not the overwhelmed part, but rather the feeling of being overwhelmed. That feeling is one of claustrophobia, suffocating under my burden.

I create this feeling. Part of me wants to feel claustrophobic, wants the motivation of escaping from such suffocation.

In a subtle way, the feeling of overwhelmed is creating motivation. I motivate myself by focusing on how to escape suffocation. . . and ultimately, death.

Going deeper, is the overwhelmed feeling based on the fear of death? Am I creating this fear in order to focus my mind? Probably.

By accepting and dealing with the overwhelmed feeling, I fight against sliding off the cliff, and a hurtling descent into the abyss of death.

Embrace overwhelmed. Better overwhelmed than to die. That's the concept. I agree.

A Place in the Future: Living the After-Life

If fear of death helps motivate and focus my mind in this life, would fear of life help motivate and focus me in the after life?

I'm talking here about fear of rebirth, reincarnation, and never wanting to return to this worldly material existence.

I've read about souls enjoy the after-life. Few want to return to this world. Rather than return to earth for a visit, they'd rather their soul mates and friends join them up there. "Things are good here," they say, "Real peaceful. Why would anyone want to return? A woman in Florida said, 'I should have come here years ago.' The afterlife is so relaxed and easy going. No pressures. A pleasant, non-material floating existence. This is real retirement! No worries about pension plans or social security checks. Indeed, I should have done it years ago."

Worldly people say, "Who wants death when you can have life?" But those up above say, "Who wants life when you can have death?"

Presently, I am still attached to my body. I don't want to lose it. But posthumously, I may say, "Who needs it?"

Freedom versus Peace

Freedom is obviously much more dangerous than peace. You have the freedom to succeed marvelously, but also the freedom to fail miserably; under freedom you are free to embrace life but also free to kill yourself.

Peace however, is a middle state without ups and downs. In order to maintain it, you have to push down the ups, and pull up the downs.

On the surface, peace sounds good. But in reality, there is quite a bit of force, even tyranny, in maintaining it. "Shut up. Keep things peaceful. Don't bother me!" These are often words that go with peace.

Freedom however, is often wild and wooly, directionless and chaotic, exciting and depressing.

I go for the wild ride. But I'll accept a quiet sail on the lake on weekends.

Love Motivation: Tectonic Plate Shift

Two tectonic plates meet and clash in my lower back. . . and even my left foot outer step. One plate is fear: the plate of the past, of old attitudes towards work. The other plate is love: the plate of the future and my attitude towards it.

Money and fear are deeply related. In the old plate world, they had been a prime source of motivation.

But now I am grinding that plate into oblivion: Going beyond it, I am moving toward and into the love motivation.

I feel the tectonic plates fighting, struggling, clashing, and crashing in my body. But slowly, gradually, now more rapidly, fear, terror, and trembling are sinking to the bottom. Love hasn't won yet, but it is quickly winning.

This is a historic period which I will entitle: The Great Transition of Attitudes period.

No doubt, when it is complete, my body will be cured.

Building Success Muscles

Evidently, success and overwhelmed go together. I want success. But I don't like being overwhelmed.

What to do?

Time to start building success muscles.

I can start with push-ups. Success push-ups. I place my hands on the Overwhelmed floor and push.

By learning and practicing this push, my success muscles will increase. I'll get stronger.

First I lie on the floor. Then I do my overwhelmed push-up. In doing so, I "distance" myself from overwhelmed.

Will I ever become successful in this venture? Can I ever completely eradicate Overwhelmed? It is, after all, a mental state.

Living in Success Land, while freeing myself from Overwhelmed, would be the greatest success of all!

Something to think about and work on.

Mind and Body

I carry the burdens of my world on my shoulders. That's why they hurt.

I bend and break my back under their weight and herculean labors: That why my back hurts.

I support the whole system with my legs. That's why they hurt. Ankles and feet are the closest connection to the earth. Knees wobble and almost buckle under the strain.

Even though Ma tried to shield me from danger, tried to make things easy, creating and carrying the art of Jimmy boy to the world is no easy task.

Part of me, a good part, feels that bringing my art to the people should be easy. That attitude comes, no doubt, from my upbringing.

But all my experience proves it is not easy. It is a constant and never-ending struggle. I am constantly amazed by this fact. Surprised and disappointed. It "should" be easy. . . but it is not. This is the voice and attitude of Ma stepping in to protect me, to smooth the road, to lighten the danger, to make me happy.

Well, it never works.

The struggle to be an artist, and to get recognition, is tough and never-ending. That is the true nature, the reality of life here on earth.

Although the salesman may not always an artist, the artist is always a salesman.

But it's not, "Woe is me, life as an artist is suffering; I have to be a salesman." Rather it is, "Life as an artist is tough; I am a hero for trying!"

I am subtly paralyzed with fear over this upcoming Florida Folk Dance Camp. And this, even though everything is together. But after all, I am leaping into the unknown. Just because it was a hit last year doesn't guarantee it will be the same this one. Evidently, I should be worried, concerned, get my performing energy up. And this even though everything I can think of doing is in order.

I want to be a hero.

How can you be a hero, if you are not afraid?

How can you be a hero, if you do not struggle against pain, suffering, and evil?

A hero fights fear and the devil. That's what makes him a hero.

Pains and the Future

I am beset by physical ailments I don't believe I have.

Deep down I believe they are mentally constructed and that they will, when the right idea comes, immediately and miraculously go away. Therefore, although I have these ailments and parts of my body hurt, I don't take them seriously. Part of me laughs at them, and even boasts that I am a hero because I consider them so insignificant.

Right now I ache because of the upcoming Florida Folk Dance Camp. That is the origin of my newest "folk dance ankle" pain. True, it does not seem to be in the usual place. . . or is it?   Actually, I don't really remember.   But it is, nevertheless, in the ankle area.

These pains are so "interesting."   Are any of them really new?   Haven't I had them all before?   Well, yes.   But they are nevertheless different every time.   Why?   Because the challenges, fear, angers, and terrors I face are different every time.   Take the upcoming Florida Folk Dance Camp, for example.   Last year I spend months preparing for it.   This year, I am totally prepared.   I "know" what will happen done there.   I've done it before.

Well, have I really "done" it before?   How could I have "done it" when it has not yet happened?   Aha, this a future event, and although I can prepare as much as possible—and I have—nevertheless, the future is the land of the Unknown.   And the Unknown is filled with surprises, terrors, unexpected leaps and falls.   It is the Mystery, the Unknown.   Truly, prepare as much as I might, I can never truly know what will happen.   Thus fears, doubts, hesitations haunt and even plague my mind.   As well they should.   I am facing the abyss.   No matter how much skill I have amassed over the years, there is always the chance I could fall in.   Past success does not insure future success.   Even the skills that have become so much a part of me could suddenly, for "no reason," fall away and disappear.   Anything is possible in the hidden, unknown, and distant future.

No wonder I am hesitant and afraid; no wonder my body reflects these doubts in its aches and pains.

Only awareness of their origin seems to be the cure.   And perhaps, ultimately, the only cure is to do and finish the Florida Folk Dance Camp.   Then my reality created tension will go away; the camp will be over; I can move on. . . to the next event, the next tour, the next group of tensions created by facing the future and its Unknown.

So, the pains I feel are reality based.   Yet, even though they are real, they remain insignificant in their offering.   They are like the back and gastrocnemius spasms.   They hurt like hell, terrify the soul, make you scream with pain, but, in actuality, do no physical damage to the body.   They kill the mind, but leave the body in tact.

Isn't this why a good part of me realizes their origin and truth, and thus does not take them seriously.   But they hurt so much I often doubt myself and the psycho-mental origins of these pains.

Doubt and belief stand side by side in the schizophrenic mind. Such phrenias, schizoid, even multoid, schizophrenia, even multiphrenia, may be the very nature of mind itself.

There is no escape from my mind. However, awareness of how it operates might help.

The Power of Core Values: A Scattered Explanation

True power comes from core beliefs, values, and principles. From these, even if you have no money, arms, or power, you can still start to build it.

If you have only money, but no principles, values, and core beliefs, your only power is one of appeasement: you can buy off your enemy. But the enemy keeps wanting more and more, and eventually defeats you.

Core principles however, fight from the inside. And this even without money. From core beliefs, principles, and values, outside political influence, power, and money will follow.

Ecstasy Beyond the Boundaries

I always used to push a little beyond the barrier. This sometimes created injuries, but it also led to ecstasy.

During the past year or two I have been experimenting with pulling back. I have tried restraining myself from pushing beyond the barrier, tried to be "more mature and reasonable."

Result: I have injured myself less. But I also have less ecstasy.

Is this a good thing?

Also, in spite of my "reasonable and mature" approach, my body still aches in various places.

Is this "mature" approach a good thing?

Could these vague aches be caused by restraint, by my "mature and reasonable" approach? Could this approach be fostered by a fear of injury, and subsequently, a fear of ecstasy? A fear of its dangers?

What are the dangers of ecstasy? Injury, of course. Injury hurts. It is also annoying.

Perhaps it is not maturity and reasonableness at all that keeps my from pushing slightly beyond my boundaries, but rather a subtle but growing fear of injury.

Should I fear injury? Maybe. Should I thus fear pushing beyond my boundaries? Maybe. Should I fear the giving up, the loss of ecstasy? Maybe to yes!

But I cannot have ecstasy without pushing slightly beyond my boundaries. And isn't ecstasy, ultimately, my God connection. And when I make the connection, often my injuries go away.

Thus, by holding back, I may even be creating my own injuries. Instead of free-flowing, healing energy, expressed and released by pushing slightly beyond my boundaries, and the ecstasy it creates, my energy becomes bottled-up inside me; it then turns to poison, gnaws at my muscles, and slowly destroys my body.

So it is a question of ecstasy versus fear of injury.

But another question arises: Will ecstasy cure the injuries?

I believe it will. In any case, it is worth a try.

Maybe I needed to avoid ecstasy during this transition period. I was too unstable to take a chance with it. But now stability is returning as I become accustomed to this new success place.

I am ready to take another chance, to push beyond my boundaries, to heal my injuries, aches, and pains by regenerating the powerful juices of divinity, the sparks, fire, and cosmic dynamism of energy-flowing ecstasy.

Ecstasy is definitely what has been missing from my life during this transitional period.

During this period of mental, physical, and even spiritual growth, strange new pains have appeared in my shoulders, legs, ankles, and other parts of my body. Even my lower back hurts a bit.

These could all be pains of restraint. A wise mental and physical holding back while my slow transition formed my new body to fit my new mind. Don't take chances while crossing a shaky bridge to the new land. But now, as I become more comfortable and established in my new home, I am ready to bring some of my old luggage across the bridge, bring back some of the jewels I left behind. Ecstasy is one of them.

Will ecstasy cure or hurt me?

Both.

It cures me as it hurts me. And it hurts me as it cures me.

Self-Cure Through Root Canal Therapy

My root canal, upper molar therapy session with Dr. Jerome lowered my resistence. But it may also have been lowered by my realization that "fast and fluid" guitar playing is easier.

I like the idea of connecting "fast and fluid," to root canal, and my sore throat which began an hour after Dr. Jerome's session.

How and what is the connection? How are "fast and fluid," root canal, and sore throat related?

Well, the shock of freedom that "fast and fluid is easier," plus the added shock of root canal therapy, lowered my resistence, and opened me to sore throat germs.

Why the throat? Such marvelous "fast and fluid" freedom, in both guitar playing and in life, may be "unspeakable."

Also I may have chosen sickness to replace the joy of such wonderful freedom. I don't know if this analysis is right. But I do know, I would like to believe it is. Such a belief would give me understanding and control over my sore throat.

There is a good chance I am right.

Even if I am wrong, thinking in this manner releases positive energy into the veins which help cure me.

Regrouping

Very interesting, psychologically. I have been trying to figure out why I no longer exercise, run, do yoga, or, if I do it, I do it so minimally. Well, this morning it came to me: I have been pulling back, mentally and physically, for the past year or two, in order to regroup.

My army, my forces, both mental and physical, have been knocked out of wack. A new balance of power has to be established. First comes shock and awe, then stunned, then slow recovery to figure out where I am, then wondering which direction to turn, and, in the process, I wait, pull back, hold myself in abeyance. I am thus in the process of regrouping my forces.

When I can figure out my new direction (the process sometimes takes months, even years), then my army will return with full force to fight in the next miracle schedule battle.

The regrouping process cannot be rushed. I cannot force myself to exercise, run, do yoga, whatever. Why? Because half my brain is in the old world and the other half is trying to figure out my next direction into the new. I am thus in an extended limbo state.

My brain is in conflict, paralyzed, waiting, puzzling, and in the process of deep changes. It is folly to fight against it.

Rather, let the process run its course. Soon all will be revealed. Then I will return to my renewed miracle schedule but on another level.

The Old Jim Gold is Dead and Gone

I can't go backwards. The past is over. I can't go back to the old miracle schedule. The old miracle schedule is dead!

I can only go forward into the future. That means I will need an entirely new miracle schedule. It might even need a new name. I might even have to eliminate the word "miracle" and "schedule."

I may have to start all over.

Miracle Schedule is dead. That may be part of the problem. I have been living with a corpse. And, in partially realizing it is a corpse, I have been partly trying to resurrect it.

Well, this will never work. One cannot resurrect an old dead body. One needs a new fresh body along with a new mind to boot! On the way, a new name will be born.

Is this goodbye to the miracle schedule life? Maybe. No wonder I have been stiff, paralyzed, unable to move. No wonder bones and body ache with stiffness. My spirit has been dwelling in a mind that is brain-dead, and a body that is a corpse.

Spirit needs a new home, a new body and mind in which to dwell.

The old Jim Gold is dead and gone.

I wonder when the new one will appear.

Onwards and Inwards

Some brand new ideas might be:

1. Join the master's running club that meets Tuesday night at the Teaneck High School track.

2. Master to Torah and bible. . . in Hebrew. . . (and later even the New Testament in Greek? Would this mean an eventual tour to Greece, and Israel? But with a different scholarly (non-folk dance, or less folk dance, emphasis) purpose.

Is a Spark Worth Keeping?

Reflections on the Terry Schiavo case: How much is life worth, if you are worthless? How much are you worth, if you become a burden to others? In this "worthless" state, are you really a burden to others? Or could you be a symbol of a heavy learning, an instrument of difficult and painful teaching?

In that final state, are you worthless? Or is the pain of your existence and the sorrow it causes others, simply "too much" for them to bear? Hoping not to face it, others might simply have you die.

If I am totally incapacitated, in final pre-death state, and I lie helpless, a pain to myself and a burden to others, would I prefer death over days, months, (even years) of such a "useless" existence?

Maybe. Yet this spark of life hanging on in a dying body is, nevertheless, all I've got. Is it worth anything? Is my state useful in any way? Could it ever be a worthy teaching to others, opening up some higher learning about the nature of life and death?

Would I want to live, "exist," in such a state? Would others want me to? Aside from practical questions of the cost to keep "vegetables" alive, do members of this legume family have any value to society? Good questions, indeed.

Bible Study

I have a long-term goal of reading the Bible. First I study the Old Testament in both Hebrew (and Bulgarian, or whatever other language I am learning.) Then (if I ever reach that point in this life time),

I will read the New Testament in the original Greek.

This is a great goal of linguistic, intellectual, and scholarly expansion. I love the quiet, focused study, the deep learning process. Language books, grammars, and dictionaries are spread over my dining room study table. I jump from one book to another looking for roots, origins, and meanings of new foreign words. Ah, such stimulation and such fun! What an adventure!

Actually, this Bible-reading is an old goal. But I gave it up for many months, nay years, in my all-consuming leap into business. Now perhaps I am ready to give it some time. My best time, morning time. First thing in the morning, cup of coffee sitting to my right, I begin my bible studies.

These could be followed by writing, guitar, exercises, whatever. After that, I move to my desk and computer to dive into the boiling world of sales, promotion, and business.

Bible study. A good reason to get up 5:00 a.m.

Money and Its Breathren

Market

Fear is stronger than greed. That's why the market falls faster than it rises. Shorts will make money "faster" than longs. But, of course, the art is in the timing!

Money symbolizes connection to others. Ultimately, that's what sales and service is all about.

Crazy for Stocks; Crazy for Trading

I'm looking at shorts and charting. Am I crazy? I used to think that shorting stocks was the height of gambling and, in general, really bad for a moral person. Where did I get such an idea? Who knows? But it is based on ignorance.

What about charting? That too, I thought, was only used by morons and dreamers, stock pickers and traders whose minds were in the sky, lost in dreamland, naive, believers in predicting the future. I also read that technicians (as opposed to fundamentalists) never made money. Their charting and charts were silly and lead nowhere.

Now I'm getting interested in charts and charting. Indeed, I am crazy. But what does crazy mean to me? Why, of course, it means divine madness, crazy with passion! I like crazy. It is, in my mind, a higher state. Perhaps the highest. It is the one closest to God.

Check out this *New Leaf*. What's its title? Passion! Evidently, I have a passion for stocks. And for money. I don't know why they intrigue and excite me, but they do. Truth is, I don't care about the "Why?" I'm just glad about the "do." To me, trading is the most exciting, challenging, the highest form of dealing with stocks.

Witnessing the Stock-Flowing Moment

This morning it seems the market will go up. . . and I love it.

A few hours ago it seemed the market would go down. . .and I hate it.

Am I capable of a more balanced approach?

Do I even want one? Isn't emotionalism part of the fun? Yes, but so far, only when the market goes up. I am still caught between panic and fear on the one side and excitement, exhilaration, triumph, and victory cries on the other.

Well, all this gives me lots of good writing material, but I doubt it will solve the problem. Again I should look to the artistic approach for faith. Are there stock market artists?

Meanwhile I might as well enjoy this brief up moment. That is the Zen-like answer: Enjoy the moment. Live in the moment. But realize it is precisely that: a moment. Moments change. They are part of the infinite Flow. My job is to enter the flow and witness it as well.

Energizing Aspects of Fear

I've been doing well in the stock market during the past week. My account and my stocks have been in the green gain column. I've even made a little money.

Paradoxically, part of me misses the energizing worry, the energizing fear of the red loss column. Once again I recognize the energizing aspects of fear. Paralyzing fear, panic, is an awful feeling. But a tinge of worry, a touch or "pinch" of fear, often acts as a stimulant. A pinch of pepper in your food wakes you up, makes you alert, focused, on guard, and ready for action.

Money

Hold my stocks for six months to a year. Short term.

Even though the past few weeks have been good, my stocks have gone up and I've made money, nevertheless, remember: I am still a beginner. My next stage starts in November, 2003. That will make one year of entry and study of the market on my own, We'll see by then if I can make money on a consistent basis.

How to measure consistent? Not by making money every day but every week. This pushes me past the daily wiggles (two to five days) of the market.

Maybe I should look at my totals every week instead of every day. Say every Monday morning.

I also like the definition of a professional trader by Toni Turner: "Commit to consistently take profits out of the market.

By November, 2003 I should know more. So far during the first six months of trading I've lost money. A few weeks ago the second six months began. The tech market (and the market in general) is going up. I started to make money. We'll see where this takes me.

Stock Speculation

Can playing the stock market be a good-in-itself.

Are you kidding? How could that happen? The world of stock market, manipulation, gambling, money, as goods-in-themselves? Aren't they evil parts of the lower, sinful world?

Can the process of stock speculation ever be a good thing? Can I ever take pride in it? Can anyone? How about folks like Jesse Livermore?

Maybe you can take pride in your skills. But how about the stock market speculation process itself? Can that be good? What would mother say?

And how about all the other communists? What would they say? Surely, if I think this way, I will be expelled from the Party. No good communist would ever embrace "gambling," much less such any aspect of the capitalist system.

Maybe a good can be found in stock speculation. But so far my upbringing and background disable me from seeing it.

Another Stock Market Juncture

I realize I will never use the money I make (or lose) in the stock market to support myself. If I make money, it will simply go back into the market; if I lose money, well, hopefully I won't lose too much. Still, even my losses will not effect my life style. They will stay in the market.

Thus the stock market is a speculative trading game I like to play.

Where does it fit into my life? Is it part of the miracle schedule? I doubt it. Is it part of business? No.

What is it? I like the challenge, risk, and adventure of playing it.

Still, why spend so much time and effort and mental energy on this up and down "meaningless" game? Wouldn't I be better off spending my time developing aspects of my miracle schedule?

Originally, I got into the market because I wanted to make money, get rich, and ultimately, free myself from financial fears so I could be and practice my arts in peace. Well, I am practicing my arts in peace. On that I have succeeded. Yet I remain in the market. And it is not even to make money for my real life.

I am in the market mainly to win; I would like to "conquer" it. I measure my wins by the amount of money I make; I measure my loses by the amount of money I lose.

But ultimately, am I not wasting my time?

May was a great month. I made money. I won. June has been a terrible month. I lost money. I lost. Today when I ad up my gains and losses, I see I have lost more money than I have made. Thus the results of all my trading effort so far have moved from zero to minus zero. I have, in a sense, gone nowhere.

Maybe I've learned something psychologically.

In any case, I'm at another stock market juncture.

"Different Feel" in the Stock Market

Yesterday the torturous month of June holding of my stocks paid off. Not only did they return to even (after being down almost $7000) but they went up! This morning I am happy and proud of myself for having the courage (and foresight. . . wow, dare I say such a word!) to have held on during the down month. I put all my stop losses at ten per cent below each stock. . . just in case. (One must always use stop losses!) But my long range view, that the market is heading up, paid off.

Loving the Study!

Perhaps I play the stock market with such hope-filled intensity to fill my emptiness. I need excitement. And I love to study.

Perhaps the stock market and its excitement have little to do with money. (Although winning would be nice.)

Rather it is fundamentally about emptiness, learning, and the excitement of study! We Jews love to study.

Without something new and exciting to pursue, life gets bland and energy drains away. Most of the meaning goes out of it.

For over a year the stock market filled my mind with excitement, goals, and love. It was the game of learning and the joy of study, that I pursue.

Relief: Out of the Market

I hate to admit it but its such a relief being mostly out of the market. It's a feeling of control. Plus I have something I never had even when I was winning: inner peace!

I have been through a one-year stock market passage. Even though I have a lot less money through the market, and have given up the idea of making any future money in it, what a burden has been lifted off my head! Perhaps I am poor, in debt. . . but unburdened! And this, for the first time. Free!

Wild, indeed. I never would have expected these feelings of inner freedom. Is this what graduation, giving up hopes, and realism is all about? If yes, give me more of it!

The stock market is okay as a miniature sideline, play thing. . . very minor plaything. The less time I put in it, the better I feel. But the important thing to remember is: I felt enslaved, haunted, even obsessed by it whether I was making money or not. Amazingly thus, the money was besides the point. When I was riding high in early September making 1G a day, I couldn't shake it; and when I was down in the dumps losing 1G a day, I couldn't shake it.

Only now, by giving up all my hopes, have I shaken it.

Stock Market

How empty and out of it I felt after I sold all my stocks before leaving for Prague and Budapest. How empty and depressed I felt after I sold my stocks last May before leaving for Spain. Sure the pre-Spanish selling it turned out to be the right decision. I would have lost much more had I stayed in. Also I couldn't trade from Europe. It enabled me to finally get out of trading with Joel. Ultimately, was able to go off and trade on my own. It was a major break and initiated the end of one trading era, and the beginning of a long transition into the new one.

But the underlining theme of all this was my love of trading. It's excitement, unpredictability, intrigue, horrific runs of downs, elating times of ups, and a general feeling of passionate involvement. These are big words, big concepts.

True, part of me feels guilty for this love. That's because I lost so much money in it. But more than that, it's because I get chewed out about it. Sure I don't like to be yelled at or criticized especially when I have been wrong in the market, lost money, and am vulnerable. I feel double bad: bad for losing and bad for being criticized about losing.

But nevertheless, I keep returning to the market. Sure, some may call this a gambling disease, a sickness, irresponsible, a daredevil's lack of care. All this may be true. But . . . I don't care. I simply love and need the market.

June had a nice comment about Tom's market playing: "It's good for him. It gives him something to do with his mind." Now true, Tom has plenty of money and losing some of it is not a threat to him. Even though I don't have plenty of money, nevertheless, the basic truth is the same: It is a game that fills my mind with something exciting and challenging to do.

And there is also the possibility that I'll get better at it. I might even make money!

Make money, lose money, that is the nature of the game. But most important is the realization that: I love, need, and want to play!

Ploughing Full Speed Ahead Growing JGI

I'm giving up the stock market. I have a huge debt. Is there any place for hope?

If I don't have the market, and my tours don't work out, or at least, if my hopes for making any money in tours are at a low, then where can I find hope?

How can I, alone, pay off this huge debt?

Of course, truth is, I have always been alone. Only I "hoped" I would get help, first from my tours, then the market, then both.

If I give up the market (and with it my hopes), and if tours do not pan out, it will take me years to pay this thing off. Years! Maybe until the rest of my life.

And I only have me to rely on.

Strangely, part of me feels relieved to be getting out of the market. But this morning, part of me also feels a slight panic about the deep hole I am in.

Well, even as I stand now at the bottom of the pit, part of me tries to find something positive in this mess. There must be some pluses to such a minus situation. Would I call this a basic and fundamental optimism in my personality? Maybe. Plus, I can't stand living without hope. Does that make my hopes realistic? Can I really put total faith and hope in myself? Of course, I have no other choice.

Well, moving beyond this philosophical rambling, what exactly could be positive?

1. I'll be fully concentrating on making money in my business, on promoting every and all products of JGI. I'll not spend a moment of mental energy hoping that the market will go up and subtly, in Mommy and Daddy fashion, save me from bankruptcy and debt. Yes, I said it: bankruptcy. At the moment, I'm not choosing that option. (But I did say the word.) Instead, I'm choosing to keep my credit (and good name) and pay everything off. Slowly. How slowly? Maybe years slowly. But time is not the question here; hope is.

2. By fully concentrating on my business, on building up JGI in all its aspects, I could, eventually, actually make money! And in the process, I would be bringing public all the products and services I have worked so hard over the years to perfect. Even folk dancing and folk dance classes might make money. If I put the right kind of time and effort into them. And from this folk dance base, again I could promote, once again, my weekends, tours, and even more.

Plus there is the other aspect of my business: bookings. These could also be promoted in class and beyond.

3. During the past few months I have been looking for a new challenge. Well, I have found it! But my bottom line challenge has been to face my greatest nemesis: my resistence to sales and marketing. Well, now I have no choice but to face it. Plus, part of me wants to face it. Or to put it another way, I am very frustrated: after having worked all these years to finally believe in myself as an artist, now I want to get the word out. My excellent books sit in my basement, my excellent tours have small to no attendance, my dance classes are small, my concert booking are rare (klezmer bookings are not bad, but that is because of Michele's efforts). Thus all my talents remain out of public reach, and "in the closet." This has always been a major, maybe the major frustration for me. But the rejection and annoyance of sales, of pushing and marketing all my service and products, has always kept from doing the necessary sales work. I have always had that deep communistic resistence to, ugh, marketing my products. Plus, I also needed time to develop them. But now, all that is over. The products and services are fully developed. I have, artistically, done everything I wanted to do in life. The development phase is at an end. I am ready for something new.

Well, I now have it!

Part of me feels a touch of panic. But part of me may, nay will be, energized. On the one hand, I have no choice but to do this. On the other hand, part of me will eventually be glad I have finally been forced, or am ready, to face my biggest monster: the sales and marketing nemesis.

Is this why God wanted me to lose my money and go into debt? Was this His miserable, painful way of teaching me? Of course, without pain, I probably wouldn't listen. And I haven't listened for at least twenty-five years.

But I am listening now. I am ready.

And ironically, I am choosing to listen. Truth is, I could still decide to stay in the market. I could also decide that somehow, magically, my tours and JGI business could and will succeed without supreme sales efforts from me. I could decide to remain in the floaty world of magic and supernatural hope.

But I have decided not to. Why now? Evidently, I am in a new place: I am ready.

Performance

Power of the Audience

Helping others often happens subtly, and in such a "selfish" manner, that it is not recognized.

As I practice guitar trying to improve "for myself", in the back of my mind is a future performance for an audience. Thus, my practicing is, ultimately, "for them."

I have been trying to cure this problem for years. Now I see it as the core of being human, a fundamental part of existence. Luckily, it is incurable. Attempts to cure it should never be made in the first place. The desire to perform for the audience, ever remembering its mysterious powers, is my big secret.

Searching for the Perfect "Leyenda"

I am hesitant, nay, afraid, to practice slowly, to focus deeply on this meditative relaxation with the "Leyenda" barre as well as the "Zapateado," "Alhambra" tremolos.

I touch the deepest levels of relaxation.

I fear to touch these deep levels, and restart my search for perfection. Yet I am doing it.

Vince says, "Aim for perfection. Settle for excellence along the way." I like my hesitancy on the search. It energizes me, give me hope. Sure I'll "settle" for excellence along the way but I'll keep searching for that perfect "Alhambra", that perfect "Leyenda", that perfect tremolo and arpeggio. One illusion is aim to achieve perfection. No! Perfection can never be achieved. Only in death do we achieve it, and even that is questionable.

Perfection is however, the constant goal, and thus, a constant stimulant. We can achieve excellence, not perfection. Thus we stay ever in the Flow, never moving beyond it. While the left foot stands in excellence, the right foot steps forward on the road to perfection.

Talent

At yesterday's Bar Mitzvah at the Rolling Hills Country Club in Wilton, Connecticut, a hundred people got up to folk dance.

Giuseppe said to me, "It's a talent."

Yes, I've got a talent. . . with people. I can get them to dance. I can lead. It's always been "easy" for me. I hardly ever even think about it. It is the foundation of my success.

Group leadership and relationships. . . that's the talent. Peter Drucker says talent is what comes so easily, you don't even think of or recognize it as a talent. It is too natural, simply, and easy for you.

I agree.

Hypothenar Teacher

Guitar: A never-before-felt pain in the hypothenar muscle of my right thumb. It's brand new. I wonder what it means?

Is it a resistence pain? Could it have something to do with this morning's lack of interest? I doubt it. But who knows? Why did it appear today? Surely it is a teacher in hypothenar form.

What will it teach me?

Tremolo Ma

Part of me does not want to let go of the idea that I can't play tremolo and arpeggio.

Part of me has a vested interest in keeping the "I don't have it" idea.

Why do I want to keep one foot in the house of the past? What's in it for me?

The connection.

Yes, I definitely want to maintain the connection. I want to stay in touch with Ma. But can't she sanction my new, free, and competent self?

Perhaps I need a new Ma. . .or at least a new concept of Ma. Since I made her up, invented her, in the first place, perhaps it is time to make up, to invent, a new Ma.

That way I can still stay in touch.

The new Ma is born from the old. She rises like a phoenix from the ashes.

Indeed, I need a new Ma to fit my new post-transitional guitar self, one who will allow me to play tremolo and arpeggio with competence and in freedom, and to move forward in "I've got it" mode. I need an arpeggiated mother, a new tremolo Ma.

Can one love an idiot? Why not?

Rewards of Slow, Focused Guitar Playing

Somehow I've always associated speed with strength and macho. Thus in the old school of thought, by "slowing down" I am losing my strength and giving up, losing, my macho.

Is this true? No question I am losing something. But is it really strength and macho? Yes, it is part of aging to lose some physical strength. But isn't most strength psychological and mental? Macho, too?

Thus, according to this new, modern, and up to date definition, by going slow I am gaining strength. . . and macho! I could say that, in the past, I didn't have the strength and maturity of focus, to relax, to go slow. My mind was a wild horse, uncontrolled, and untamed. It went in all directions. Now I am able to rein it in, and control it. By slowing down, by accepting and even embracing the go-slow method, I take control of my mind and with it, my life.

By giving up speedy guitar playing I take command. Segovia and company are no longer running my ship. Depth, focus, and self-command win the day.

Gnostic Guitar

Thinking through the guitar, on the spot, in the moment, in the here and now, is gnostic experience.

What a gift to the audience! To present before their eyes, a thought process in motion. Making up notes, sounds, and musical phrasing on the spot. Such a radical new interpretation of "Leyenda"'s, "Alhambra"'s, and whatever.

What a radical new approach!

True, it would take courage to perform this way. But also, there is no other way.

A Different Feel

Villa-Lobos Prelude No. 1: Maybe there is a different kind of relaxation felt in the right hand finger tips.

The fast feel is different. Blood rushes to every finger tip.

It's a "different feel."

It may even be an acquired taste. Like success.

Ma Nishtanah?

This guitar "different feel" is similar to an old place I felt twenty to maybe thirty years ago. But I denied it no doubt partially due to my teacher, Alexander Bellow's improvement factor.

It is a rebirth of the old but with an important difference. Technically, that difference is in the finger tip feeling. But mentally and spiritually, the main difference is in the self-confidence factor. The twenty-to thirty-year period was not so much for technical improvement as for the revealing and building of guitar playing self-confidence.

This time around I know I am right!

It is a scary thing to say: I know I am right! But the difference now is: I am not scared!

Ma Nishtanah? That's the *nishtanah*.

The Beauty Feeling

I'm going back, singing my old yodeling songs. I keep breaking down and crying. Is it nostalgia? Is it over the beauty of singing the songs themselves? Is it both?

I avoided this sadness for years. Nevertheless, I ask the question: What am I really crying about?

Is it really nostalgia and melancholy? Or is it the long-time repression of beauty and the beauty feeling?

Am I crying for sadness. . .or joy?

Like the same tears I shed over the magnificence of Beethoven's music, these are tears of joy shed over the beauty of the music.

Part of the beauty of these yodeling folk songs in particular and folk songs in general, is the majesty of their simplicity. There is also a very close "human" connection.

All music is human. The "human" connection is again the beauty feeling coming to the fore.

Guitar

How easy the tremolos and arpeggios are moving along!

I also seem to have found a new spot in my right ring finger, a strong, confident, meaty place where the flesh meets the nail at a non-cracking point. It feels beyond the split nail effect. Its center is deep in the relaxation point of the second joint of the right ring finger. A qualitatively different place. Indeed, a Different Feel.

On My Guitar Career

Now that I have accomplished my guitar-playing artistic goals, is my career as a professional guitarist over?

Sure, I'd like to perform: "It would be nice." But if I don't put in efforts to promote and sell my performances, my bookings, then they simply will not happen. Financial need used to be my biggest motivation. But finances have long ago drifted into the folk dance field, along with running tours and weekends. Most of my bookings, too, are folk dance bookings. Truth is, dependence on money from guitar and song performances disappeared long ago. The only thing keeping it alive was my secret hope that someday, after I "improved enough," after I mastered the tremolo, "alhambra", and arpeggios, I would "return" to performing with a vengeance; I would make my comeback as an excellent, skillful, full-confidence performer.

Well, I have accomplished that goal! I am now an excellent, skillful, full-confidence performer who can also play, to my satisfaction, the tremolo, "alhambra", and arpeggios. Truth is, I was always an excellent and skillful performer. Only the confidence was lacking. Now I have supplied the confidence, too.

Thus, goal accomplished. Sure, it took over twenty years, but what's the difference.

Now what?

I no longer have any strong desire or need to promote my accomplishments, to make them pay off in money. Simply accomplishing them was enough. My dream of future artistic skills and gains is over. Now guitar, singing (always had), and perhaps even writing can take their place in the Jim Gold Pantheon. What shall this pantheon be called? The Pantheon of What Now?

Why should I bother practicing? Why should I bother singing (I don't anyway)?

I know why I write, run, or do yoga: I have to. It is solely based on an inner need. I need no public acclaim (although for writing it would be nice.)

Do I have a physical, mental, and spiritual need to play guitar or sing? Or will it go the why of the violin, disappear and die? How sad to even think it. But possible, nevertheless.

Give up the guitar?

Give up singing? (I've just about done that, anyway.)

Give up any hopes, desires, practice and preparation for future performances?

I gave up violin. I thought I never could.

Can I, should I, give up guitar, too? How sad. All that work, time, and effort. Of course, I put mucho work, time, and effort into the violin, too. I don't miss playing it at all. Will I give up guitar, will I not miss playing it either? Do I really need it, after all?

What difficult questions.

The Memory of My Creation Will Last Forever!

I did a fantastic job teaching folk dancing and playing classical guitar at the Zelda Kimball 80th Birthday party. As usual, I was nervous before the event and worked hard. Finally, it ended up a great evening. People loved it. I loved it. Lots of love here.

Zelda paid me my $600 check at the end of the night. I thanked her, pocketed it, packed, and went home. On the way home, I stopped at a deli in Englewood to buy bagels and cheese.

When I got home I dumped my wallet, car keys, watch, and right pocket contents on my desk. No check!

What! I couldn't believe it: No check! Where was it? Had I lost it? This had never happened before. Had it slipped out of my pocket when I was paying at the deli in Englewood.

I searched everywhere and found nothing.

I cried, then I hit the ceiling, furious with myself. Where was my mind? Where was my brain? I'd left it in Englewood. I had worked so hard, and no reward! I went to sleep with rage still simmering in my head.

This morning I woke up with a headache. Why do I have a headache? Why am I so upset about this annoying incident? Sure, it means I have to call Zelda, ask her to stop payment on the check and send me another. It's embarrassing to me, no fun for her, and just generally a pain in the ass.

Nevertheless, this headache is familiar. And it is not because I messed up and lost the check.

Rather, losing the check gives me a perfect reason to deny and forget the glory of the evening, what joy I gave to people, and what a great job I did!

That satisfaction is really my ultimate reward. Sure, I want and need the money. No question about that. Nevertheless, the headache and the denial of beautiful guitar playing, and folk dance leading, and general running of the evening (due to so much experience running events and being in tune with the participants) is so typical of my old neighborhood problems.

Denial of my goodness, pushing away the glory, drowning the wahoo! Typical, indeed.

Not getting my money is annoying. But I'll get it back. A temporary pain. But the glory of the evening and the memory of my creation will last forever!

My celestial compensation is the Glory, Wonder, and Satisfaction of a job well done, of bringing Beauty and dancing Joy to others.

My earthly reward is the money.

New Freedom in Left Hand Guitar Fingerings

New freedom in left hand guitar fingerings: Crossing of index (i finger) and middle (m finger) does not matter.

As seen and demonstrated in Matachin by the eighteenth century Spanish composer, Gaspar Sanz, edited by Emilio Pujol (my fingerings added) and in Six Lute Pieces of the Renaissance transcribed from the Lute tablature by Oscar Chilesotti (1848–1916) and edited by Albert Valdes Blain (also my fingerings added).

This will lead to new freedom in performing.

On the Quality and Meaning of the Right Hand Guitar Fingers

What is the difference in quality of the right hand guitar fingers?

Should I use ring (a) or middle (m) finger on the note D of the second section, eighth measure of Andante, the first of the Six Lute Pieces of the Renaissance?

I can't decide. I lean towards m because it has (can create) a sweeter tone; but I also like the naily sharper quality of the a finger.

Does it matter?

Yes!

Knowing which finger to use will make me more certain in my playing. It will free me to play with more confidence!

A definite fingering is very important. I just can't decide yet which one to use. But eventually I must decide. Each note belongs to a specific finger. There is a best choice. I just don't know what it is yet.

I'm leading folk dancing and singing at Congregation Sons of Israel in Leonia tonight. It's only 3:30 in the afternoon but I can't stop thinking about it. What to do?

I might as well enjoy the mounting intensity of this pre-performance excitement.

What did I just say?

Enjoy! Will this be my new way of looking at performances? I hope so.

On Performing Silence

On performing *Six Lute Piece Of The Renaissance*:
Silence between pieces is part of the concert presentation and music itself. Plan, it, count it, program it.

The technique, use, and power of silence at beginnings and endings of performance. Use it when playing guitar in public, teaching folk dancing, and more.

Silence, when used correctly, is extremely commanding.

Also think about meter and rhythm when performing: It's much more fun!

A Vision of Absolute Control

Since a returned from Santa Fe I see every "Zapateado," "Alhambra," "Leyenda," ("Soleares," etc.) right hand finger tip touch-and-pluck clearly in my mind. A vision of absolute control over all tremolos and arpeggios.

After hundred of years, the human mind made a qualitative lead from the Dark Ages into the Renaissance. Perhaps it is a similar slow-growth transformation process for my right hand guitar fingers.

Routine or Challenge

A routine is a warm-up.

A challenge wakens your energies and gets your blood boiling.

The "Alhambra" and "Leyenda" warm-up: slow, careful, clear, and conscious, versus the "Alhambra" and "Leyenda" challenge: fast, wild, half-muddy and half-clear, and tapping into the unconscious.

Sleep

Sometimes when I practice "Alhambra" slowly, or contemplate before a concert, folk dance class, or whatever, I fall asleep.

Such sleep is not a bad thing. It leads to darkness and rebirth.

Give in to it. See where it leads.

Slower guitar playing may equal wise guitar playing.
Is there such a thing as wise guitar playing?
Why not?
If not, why not become the first to do it?
Play wise. Wise play. Not a bad approach.
It takes a kind of personal courage; but it will certainly garner public respect.
Indeed, slow is a worthy teaching.
It also promotes awareness.

Milan "Pavane Number 2"

As I play Milan's modal "Pavane Number 2," I marvel at Bellow's excellent right and left hand fingerings. Am I arriving at an appreciation of his teaching?

This is something new. Gratitude for his teaching combined with forgiveness for his miserable, uptight, compulsive methods and personality.

But maybe, as he claimed, he was teaching the Segovia method. Although our personalities clashed (two compulsives in the same room are bound to create friction) nevertheless, maybe he got it right after all. Only I was in no position to appreciate it)

Beautiful Exactness!

There is a beautiful exactness found in Bellow's right and left hand fingerings, dynamics, and general editing.

A Dance Between Two Notes

Interpretation turns the first part of "Leyenda" into a dance between two notes: B and E with an occasional foray into the C bar which is really the note E "in disguise."

"Leyenda"

The hypnotic "Leyenda" bongs remind you of cosmic iron, the ever-present, unchanging stability of the universe. They are the ring of timelessness, the hypnotic gong (or bong) of eternity.

When I play "Leyenda," I am expressing. . . and describing, the eerie power of timeless order in everything.

"Spanish Dance Number 5" by Granados. . .and Sales

If I can play so slowly, so profoundly, and milk each delicious note out of "Spanish Dance Number 5" by Enrique Granados, what does that say about the rest of my life? Luxuriate in the moment.

Would it say anything about my attitude towards sales? Will I be able to luxuriate in each sales moment? I'd like to.

I will never be satisfied unless I aim higher, try harder, make the big effort. That is my path of fulfillment.

It is an important truth to know about myself. Could it even have been the long-term reason I created the "Alhambra" problem? "Leyenda" and arpeggio problem, too? I needed something to aim at. Subconsciously, I realized achieving my goal would bring me down. I worshiped a pagan god. In truth, the path of "Alhambra" is infinitely upward. I just have to find the next door.

Performer and Salesman

Up to now, salesmanship has been a necessary but secondary step to successful performance (getting jobs as a performer, getting customers for tours, weekends, folk dance classes, and bookings).

Performance as part of salesmanship, not vice versa.

Until now I have considered salesmanship as unartistic, uncreative, a necessary but noxious first step. The reward for eating the meal of successful salesmanship has been the bitter herb of giving my concert performance. . . or running my creative and artistic tours, weekends, etc.

But suppose I reversed the equation by seeing myself as salesman first, a salesman who performs?

In other words, the products of the Jim Gold Department Store are Jim Gold International offerings of tours, weekends, folk dance classes, bookings, *New Leaf* concerts, books sales, boutique items, etc.

I am the leading store salesman.

I become a performing salesman, a salesman whose top skill is in performance.

Performing on the spot, on the phone, in letters, in the market square, in the market place. Selling JGI products to the curious public.

Salesmanship and Performance

A great salesman is a great performer. A great performer is a great salesman. What is the difference between selling Bach partitas on the concert stage or Sears refrigerators through a great sales performance at the store, during a door-to-door sales call, or over the phone? Sure the products and sales technique are different. Otherwise both are selling.

Is sales socially accepted sadism? What about the delicious pleasure of forcing your will on someone else? The fun of convincing them you are right, and can help them?

Over and Over

From "Alhambra" and "Leyenda," to push-ups and head stands, to words, phrases, and language study, to whatever else one does: Playing, practicing, doing, performing something over and over and over and over and over and over and over and over again creates a qualitatively different feel. In so doing, it opens new doors, reveals new realities, and thus changes forever the way you do or see things.

Yes!

"Leyenda" C bar and three-fingered arpeggio: the relaxation problem is in the left hand (not the right). I can play with raised thumb, too.

This means I'm moving beyond maintenance. I can improve. I can actually become sensational! A sensational guitarist! Wow. And this physical improvement can occur "even at my age." This means such physical breakthroughs, improvements, can occur in running, yoga, fifties, calliyoga, folk dancing, all.

If the mind can conceive it, the body can (eventually) perform it. But first, the mind must believe and envision it.

The Trauma of Truth

Euphoria leads to the trauma of truth!

The trauma in "Alhambra" and "Leyenda" is knowing and absorbing the musical truth that tremolo and arpeggio melodies are in the bass.

Intellectually, I realized this a few months ago. But knowing it emotionally and in its total psychological profundity takes mucho more time.

Breaking down the doors, crashing through the barriers, often take place in a lighting flash of momentary insight. Learning to live in the new land, building, constructing the new vision "in the flesh," takes weeks, months, even years.

The Gongs of "Leyenda"

I can't believe what I see in "Leyenda."

But although I can't believe it, I see it in front of me. Ice cracks. I fall into the center of the earth. In its bowels I see the two black notes, E and B, resounding in darkness, chiming through the cosmos, gonging through the universe.

B is tension; E is resolution.

B is longer than E at the ("Leyenda") foundation of the universe. I wonder why.

Could it be to emphasize the tension. . . keep the audience awake and alive, keep the performance exciting, keep the universe on its toes?

Along with "Alhambra" and "Leyenda" comes "First Venezuelan Waltz," played *rapido* with mucho expression, then "Bulerias"!

Yes, even the lightning fast, picado "Bulerias" scales I could never do. . . but now I can. . . and am!

The Spring Sonata has come. I spring across the strings!

This is what Beyond Passion is all about.

A completely different level of breakthrough fast playing. I don't have words yet to describe it. "Breakthrough" and "fast" are old words, old and dry. For radically different new guitar-playing events, I need a new vocabulary.

How about "Picado pop-through," or "alto hieynda?"

Surely, this Beyond the Flood breakdown will affect other areas of my life: yoga, running, and even language.

The Fever Strikes

Look at my victories: Guitar, "Alhambra" and especially "Leyenda" victories. Plus I'm starting to find new, vague but future road again. The post-Florida lows are diminishing, nay, even coming to an end.

I'm touching new directions. Witness my noun collection: one word a day, my one computer move a day, even my new Yoga Techniques to Get.

But mostly it is my brilliant guitar playing. Never before have I played "Alhambra" and "Leyenda" with such fire, speed, and passion. Plus the door is opening to play all my guitar pieces in that way. Truly, a new guitar world of feverish, passionate playing is opening.

"Leyenda": Just a Few Notes!

Behind the screen of raining "Leyenda" arpeggios are just a few notes: Three gongs! Three bongs! E, B, B bars, short-lived "rest" periods of B bars coupled with C bars, B and B bars again.

In essence, "Leyenda" is only two notes: E and B.

The trees have disappeared. I see the forest.

Tie this "Leyenda" vision to the rest of my life.

Connect Singing to My Audience

When singing, look straight into the eyes of the audience, but do not focus on them. Rather as you "look" directly at them, see the notes you are singing

The notes you see will connect you to them.

Micro-Guitar Playing

Here's an experimental thought: How about applying the principles of micro-running to guitar playing. In other words, instead of warming up with the usual legatos, scales, and arpeggios, why not try warming up right away, immediate warm-ups by playing in very slow, soft and focused guitar. Micro-guitar.

The last twenty-five to thirty years of guitar practice. . .and playing, have been more about getting the "nuances."

Evidently, thirty years ago my tremolo and arpeggios were easily "adequate." But deep in my heart, I didn't believe it. I wanted to improve them. And I did. But only on a nuance level. Well, that level may have been enough. . .because it also gave me the important ingredient of confidence. Twenty-five to thirty years to get confidence. Well, perhaps time is never the question. The battle takes as long as it needs to take.

How Good

I sang "Long Journey." What a beautiful song! How magnificent, philosophical, sad, and elevating!

How could I have written such a song? How could I let such a beautiful, moving, powerful creation lie dormant for so many years? Never going public, never believing enough in myself to show or sing it to anyone?

The trauma of goodness is one of the most powerful traumas.

Is it really the trauma of how good I am? Or is it the trauma of realizing my connection to God?

What is my goodness but Goodness, and ultimately, Godness.

This feeling of union with Magnificence, of breaking down before the incredible power of its Beauty, is really the ultimate humility before the Higher Power.

Indeed, my goodness is my connection to Magnificence. And in this secular world, such mystical union with the Highest Force is misunderstood, frowned upon, looked at as crazy, psychotic, and thus its feeling, and public expression, can be a worldly danger.

But I'm going public with it anyway.

My ignorance has been to deny its overwhelming importance.

If notes are secondary in guitar playing, in dancing so are my arms and legs.

Place my mind in the dan tien. the energy center just below my navel and in front of my spine, rather than in my fingers.

Last night, with Bill and Sue, we listened to my newly issued World of Guitar CD. It made me sad because, among other things, it brought so much happiness, joy, and pleasure to Bill and Sue.

Evidently, seeing my talents in full flower, seeing how they give pleasure both to myself and others, makes me sad.

If such joy makes me sad, I wonder if sadness makes me joyful!

Why not? Such a contradiction and paradox seems "reasonable" to me. After all, if depression precedes creation, then I need to be depressed before I start creating. Creating is dynamic, fulfilling, focused, and joyful. Wouldn't I then, secretly, anticipate such joy during its preamble, my sadness otherwise called my "cosmic depression?"

Again, why not? Seems reasonable to me.

If all this is true, then joy is sadness, and sadness is joy. They are blended and mixed together. Sadness contains the seeds of future joy with it, and joy contains the seeds of future sadness with in it. We're talking her about "creative" sadness, the "depression" that precedes creation.

What about life's tragedies and woes? Could they also be counted as the sadness that precedes joy? I doubt it. But a deeper view of metaphysical truths might prove me wrong here. I hope so. But I may be stretching it.

In any case, on a creative level, there seems to be no question that sadness and joy are deeply related, two sides of the same coin, really.

If joy is sadness, and sadness is joy, then welcome them both.

The Difference Between Practicing and Playing Guitar

Practicing: I practice to improve myself, and ultimately, to change (and improve) the world. It is the "do," "doing," "to do" verb.

Playing: I play for the joy and fun of it. I try to improve or change nothing. It is the "is," "being," "to be" verb.

Which is "better," practicing or playing?

Playing is better. Why? Because even though you try to change nothing, by simply playing for the joy and fun of it, you end up changing everything! And of course, in the process of entering and embracing this egoless state, you "improve" the world!

Thus practicing precedes playing. When practicing, you are still on the road to somewhere. When playing, you are there!

Keep practicing. Why? Eventually, you'll be able to play.

I'm pretty good on the guitar. Therefore, I ought to play. On days I can't play, I can practice.

What should I practice?

Playing.

Where is my guitar going?

After a short warm-up, I am immediately playing the pieces, easy, warm-up pieces. Like Milan Pavanes. And I am interpreting them! I am working on presentation and imagination. I picture the 16th century court of Spain, kings, queens, princes, princesses all dancing slowly and majestically to the music of Luis Milan's Pavanes.

Then on to Farruca. . .and "alhambra" in the same way.

Fast and Fluid as a Life Style

VL "Prelude No. 4." It's so incredibly easy. And I've done it all before. This is the form of "deepening," of "returning to the past in depth."

Fast and fluid on "Alhambra" and "Leyenda," too.

Notice my back is better.

Fast and fluid: Does it work as a body cure in general? Probably. What about folk dancing? Does it mean the fast and fluid "Romanian-type" dances are best for me; best for my kind of body/mind, physical and mental type? Probably.

Can my Guitar Playing be Improved?

How can I go further on the guitar?

Am I at the point where only self-examination and self-exploration will work? Will discoveries and learning only take place through practice, introspection, and meditation upon what I am playing? (Such as today's "alhambra" practice "discovery" of the separation between thumb and fingers.)

Or are there books to read, places to go, other guitarists to talk to? I don't know.

It seems I'm at the point where only self-examination will lead to improvement. But I could be wrong. Perhaps there are others out there. . . .

Do I even want to step beyond myself? Or do I want to stay in this enclosed "self" world, practicing pieces over and over again until I get them right?

Musical Interpretation

Can I find a new musical direction in interpretation of these pieces?

Is interpretation a skill, or a direction? Is it worth the effort? Is it even an effort? Or is a talent, an outgrowth of natural exuberance expressed once you technically master the piece?

Is interpretation part of technical mastery or is there a false separation between technique and interpretation?

Of course, musical interpretation does concern itself with depth. And deepening is the direction in which I have recently been going.

Also, I really have no other choice. I have no interest in learning new pieces. I have too many old ones sitting unused by the wayside. How can I rescue them from oblivion? Through interpretation.

Can one study interpretation. . . or practice it? It is, on one level, so easy.

What is the challenge? What is there to practice? On the other hand, I have nothing left to do.

Musically, it seems to be the only way.

What is interpretation but expression of self. In order for it to grow and develop, one must know more about the self. This comes through life experience. No need to "practice" this.

I want a challenge. I need to grow.

Interpretation seems to be no challenge at all. Or is it? Can I make it one? Or does it fall into my lap simply by default?

Guitar

I have defeated the tyranny of speed.

I've made my peace my guitar.

No more playing in the shadow of Segovia. Slow and gravitas now belong to me!

"Get personal satisfaction by running the best tour possible with focus and concentration." I am now transferring this concept to the guitar: "Get personal satisfaction by playing the best guitar possible; play with total focus and concentration. This is best done through "slow and gravitas."

New Touch and Tone

Touch and tone are part of expression.

Playing "St. Louis Tickle," I am using a soft, relaxed, over-the-sound-hole touch.

A new, beautiful, sweet, even tone results. In the process, a new form of guitar self-expression is developing.

This new touch expresses tranquility and beauty.

Is it the beginning of a new, creative guitar road to self-expression?

B'simcha and Zoom!

The "Alhambra" *b'simcha*. (Yes, I missed most of the notes; but what a great time I had!)

And what is more important? Playing all the notes right, or *b'simcha?* At this point in my life, after so many years of practice, there is no question it is *b'simcha*. I deserve it! "Alhambra" zoom! God, is that fun!

"Leyenda" zoom. . . just as much fun!

So is Jota zoom!

Goodness

I played guitar and taught/led folk dancing at the Joanna and Peter Strauss Anniversary yesterday. Superb.

Here's the post- letter Joanna sent me:

"Dear Jim,

Tired as we are, I wanted to email you first to say how thrilled we were with your contribution to our very exciting afternoon. You were so adept and wonderful—and reawakened my somewhat dormant love of folk dance. So I'm keeping my fingers crossed that Bailey Farms appealed to you, especially the potential dance hall—and/or that the temple choir director might get the temple revved up again to folk dance (as in days of yore).

As I mentioned at the close of the evening, you received many compliments—and we're delighted that I managed to turn this fantasy of mine into a reality.

Thank you so much,

Warmly

Joanna and Peter too"

Why must I go through so many hours, nay days, of pre- anxiety in order to be superb?

Anxiety is my personal technique of getting in touch with and calling up my energy. Although during bookings I usually teach folk dancing for only about half an hour, I put a tremendous amount of. focus and concentration into getting the people to stand up, get in a circle, and start dancing. Mentally, I create a powerful ray of energy that I consciously (and unconsciously) project into each person present in the room. I focus on all of them simultaneously, creating a group unity in my mind. Then, when I ask them to dance, I project my energy straight into their hearts. Through this subtle form of projection I urge them to get up and dance.

The need to create this performing energy may be the reason I feel so much pre-anxiety. Anxiety is my engine.

New Guitar Playing

All my new guitar playing, even "Leyenda," "Alhambra," "Farruca," the flamencan dances, "Jota," luxurious "Caprichio Arabe," and more, is slower, deeper, more thoughtful; each phrase is milked for its uniqueness, inner dynamic, and beauty.

"Farruca" is the prototype of a new and future guitar playing style. It is based on slow, thoughtful, unique, dynamic interpretation, the true discovery and expression of my own style.

Rather I am using what I know in the service of interpretation and self-expression.

These are fruits of a post-transitional world I now live in.

Motivation

The anticipation that I will one day perform it publically is my ultimate motivation.

One day I will stand before my audience. I will perform well. I won't be humiliated.

I want to excel before others. I want their admiration, love respect, and approval. The universe may not care about this. But I do.

This approach shows how vulnerable I am to the fickle opinions of others.

It keeps me on the abyss of fear and humiliation. But my place at the abyss keeps me motivated. Although uncomfortable, it is not a bad place to be especially when you consider that the alternative is vitiated energy and alienated deadness.

Since motivation is energy, and connection to audience energizes me, then use this mental image in all my endeavors. Visualize an audience as I do my push-ups, sit-ups, etc.

Audience is a form of energy. Since I am connected to them, and they are connected to me, focusing on them means focusing on my energy.

I practice squats to get strong.

Why do I want to get strong? So I can show off in front of my dancers! I'll do Russian squat steps, or *Tsamikos* leaps, squats, and back bends. They'll admire me.

This is also true for my push-ups, sit-ups, scorpions, head-stands, and other yoga postures. I want to get more flexible and stronger so that I can say: "See how strong and flexible I am. See how good I am. Admire me."

If this is the fundamental source of my motivation, go for it!

Death and Rebirth is Exhausting

It's exhausting to let your old body, mind, and even the attitudinal parts of the spirit die. The follow up process of rebirth is also exhausting.

Is the process "sickening" as well?

Probably.

I am being reborn into a Flowing "Alhambra"; I am entering the Garden of "Leyenda" and, through loose and flowing flamencan piccados, joining my fish scale primordial ancestors.

New Guitar-Playing Art Form

I must remember I am an American playing Spanish classical and flamencan music. Thus I can never play them as an authentic, ethnic Spaniard. My style of playing both flamencan and Spanish classics is an American style; or perhaps a hybrid American-Spanish style. As such, it is a totally new art form.

It is an American art form, a Bronx, Jewish, American, educated, studied, synthesized, unique American art form.

I am an American teaching ethnic foreign folk dances, developing and teaching them through an American style. I am also an American playing Spanish classical guitar and especially flamencan gypsy guitar music. I am not a gypsy (although in my heart I often wonder), I am not a Spaniard (although in my heart I often speak Spanish).

Yet, when I play, because of my background and training, I am creating an Americ-Jimgoldo new guitar-playing art form. Accept it. Relish it. Luxuriate in it.

Guitar Thanksgiving

In the past few days, I have been playing better than I ever played in my whole life! Loose, relaxed, no pressure, no worry, no sense of audience watching, no sense of others judging, slow, easy, with total feeling and expression.

One cannot "practice" such a blessed state. It is more accepting a gift that has been finally bestowed upon me (from above). It is a Guitar Thanksgiving.

Miracle Spot

Is there a miracle spot?

In guitar playing, that spot is somewhere beneath my right shoulder.

It is the deepest of relaxation spots, a spot really beyond relaxation.

It is a flowing spot, a place in the body where, when you focus, the world opens up. Isn't it similar to the biblical makom kadesh," the Moses spot?

While playing guitar over the years, I have often touched on this spot. I have never been able to stay there very long. Now I am ready to stay longer.

Why Knock the Dead?

By rethinking the past, performing and singing "old" songs, recreating old thoughts and memories, you give them new life. Reborn. The dead rise and live again! You turn past into present, dream into reality.

Why knock the dead? They have their own kind of reality. And who says they're not singing anymore?

"Alhambra" Chi: I am not thinking about the notes as I play. Rather, I am thinking about dan tien, arms (and legs) relaxing, body relaxing, Chi flowing. . .but not the notes.
Chi is primary; notes are secondary.
Is this true in running, too? Legs and muscles are secondary. Relax them. Chi focus is primary.

The Notes, Indeed, are Secondary

Guitar: In this kind of Chi practice, the notes, indeed, are secondary. Focus on Chi. The notes are secondary.
That is the practice.
This kind of constant focus on Chi (the Center of the Universe) is, indeed, the Next Level.

Nervous Hypothenar Reflections

I'll be performing on the guitar at Florida Folk Dance Camp. I'm now working on, revising and looking at Serenade by Joachim Malats. Hypothenar fears are entering my right hypothenar muscles again. The advantage I have this time is one of awareness: I've been through this before. It reflects my upcoming anxiety.
Well, why shouldn't I be nervous? Indeed, I should be. This kind of nervousness for an upcoming challenge is good for me.

Pre-anxiety, and the aches and pains it creates, are all part of the performance. In other words, the starts with and includes pre- anxiety. This kind of "performance" can last days, weeks, even months.

Pre- anxiety is a knotted ball of energy. It tortures and inspires. But, no doubt, it is all part of the show, the ninety per cent of the iceberg the audience does not see.

When I woke up in Sarasota my back was killing me. I had a dream. "Tiger in the window, no money in Hungary, forgotten my money belt."

What is the psychological cause of this pain? What is the dream revelation? It must be success! It was a great Weekend, a successful Florida Folk Dance Camp. I gave it my all, my absolute best!

I met the challenge in every possible, every best, way. I ended up exhausted, but happy.

Total Weekend focus and concentration!

What is success? Becoming your own hero.

I faced the Tiger in my dream. It finally went away, disappeared. I faced it . . .and I won!

The Tiger is my back ache. I faced him, fought, and ultimately, won. I am my own hero.

The struggle of life against death: Death is the Tiger. Life is the fight to achieve a temporal win.

The fight is forever.

While fighting, worship your inner hero.

Pat your hero on the back. It's a good way to heal lower back pain.

New Musical Place

My guitar tone has turned sweet, mellow, sensuous, sensual, luscious, and beautiful. Technically, I moved my right hand over the sound hole. Emotionally, I am moving to a new place.

Power of the Audience

Helping others often happens subtly, and in such a "selfish" manner, that it is not recognized.

As I practice guitar trying to improve "for myself", in the back of my mind is a future performance for an audience. Thus, my practicing is, ultimately, "for them."

I have been trying to cure this problem for years. Now I see it as the core of being human, a fundamental part of existence. Luckily, it is incurable. Attempts to cure it should never be made in the first place. The desire to perform for the audience, ever remembering its mysterious powers, is my big secret.

The famous guitarist, performer, and composer Fernando Sor, who slept in a bathtub to keep his notes clean.

Repetition

Breaking barriers through repetition.

Recuerdos de Sevilla five-finger tremolo and arpeggios over and over and over. It takes a tremendous amount of focus power, energy, effort, and rest. Three, six, ten times more. Use repetition for yoga, and learning Photoshop. It will deepen any skill.

The secret of repetition is that it is not really repetition.

Every time your repeat, you explore a new level or layer of reality. On the surface, it may seem you are doing the same thing over and over again. But on the deepest level, it is actually impossible to repeat anything. In the stream of time and change, every action is painted with difference.

Repetition is another word for deepening.

Guitar: The Bottom Line is now Passion

I played guitar in public at Bartok's house.

Slowly, quickly, it didn't matter. No concern about tremolo or arpeggio techniques. All notes have coalesced.

The bottom line is passion.

Writing down my thoughts is a need. Sure, it's nice to publish. But it is secondary. The primary reason I write is to explain myself to myself and clear my mind.

This morning that mind is looking at soft, fast arpeggios with open focus on the base alone. The treble "relaxes" and goes along for the ride.

Tremolo and Arpeggio

The bass is the powerful, rich, and elegant melody.

The treble is the distant echo, the gray shadow against the brilliant light, the soft, gray, subtle contrast against the powerful dominant sky.

Knowing this is why I'm calm at the center. . . and happy.

Business

New Business Opportunities

Open JGI "offices" all over the country.
Start with:
1. Sasha in MA
    a. Tours and boutique items
2. Beverly in CO
    b. Draw from her Denver folk dancers and friends
3. Sally in Leonia
    a. Nursing tour
    b. Synagogue, too.

A second idea is to do something bookwise with Adam. I don't know what that is yet. Perhaps promoting my tours by selling his journals. This would also coordinate with the above "new business opportunities". All future JGI office people have Adam's Shaman and Hungarian Heritage journals.

Putting my money and efforts into human capital. Spreading JGI throughout the country. It would also help sell *New Leaf*, my other books, Adam's journals, Full Court Press, and more.

These ideas are exciting.

Adam and Gabriela would be involved, too. Even Slavik. . . the next generation. A "going public" expansion of premier order! Breakthrough at last!

I can start my physical comeback with a diet revolution!
I have to get in shape for the next twenty-year battle.

Bound to Succeed and Make Money

With this new approach I am bound to succeed and make money too. Thus, in a sense, with this new attitude, my money worries are over. How do I feel about that?

JGIO as a Motivating Force

Yesterday, mentally, verbally, and writing-wise, I moved beyond my transition. I crossed the border and stepping into JGI "Office" mode. JGIO.

If this is all true, then how does and will it effect my daily and future life? How, for example, will it effect my miracle schedule?

Could JGIO now become a motivating force, usurping the role of fear, anxiety, and dread and replacing it with enthusiasm for JGIO expansion and growth?

Could yoga, calliyoga, and running now be used and inspired by the goal of "getting and staying in shape in order to fight the JGIUO growth battle? In other words, it would imbue my mind with new purpose, place it on a new outward-inward road, fire it with enthusiasm for this new twenty-year growth and development program.

This all feels like the "next step," then one coming after last September's Cape Cod discovery of JGI Love.

Actually, JGIO is JGI Love gone public, JGI Love expanded.

But the central part for now has to be developing and expanding my tour customer base. Tours are the meat and excitement of this operation. They pay the most money; they are the kickers. Everything else is "on the side." But "sides" are important, too.

Sasha is and represents my starting point. She runs a business. So, in a sense, do the other people on this Budapest and Prague tour. Sally and Beverly especially. First, they have experienced this tour. They "know" it; they can, through their knowledge and enthusiasm, help promote the product.

How about other aspects of my miracle schedule? How will JGIO expansion effect language study? Will it rekindle my linguistic interest? We'll see.

How about guitar and writing? I'd like a new start in these areas as well. Will JGIO be the kicker? We'll see.

My Sales Staff

It means getting on the phone, taking personal time and effort, and calling these people!

These people are important to me.

Who are "these people?" They are my unpaid and unofficial sales staff.

They are connected to me and thus, an expansion of my soul.

"Going Public" is an Expansion of Self

"Going public" simply means expanding my soul. It also means extending and expanding my miracle schedule beyond myself. Outer and inner is an illusion. Since the world is my creation, "going public" really means I am expanding myself.

There is no dichotomy between art and business. Business is an expansion of self, and of my miracle schedule, too.

Sales Staff Development

We are all connected.

By expanding my dreams, I help expand the dreams of others.

By extending my soul, I help extend the soul of others.

Starting point for my sales staff should be next year's Budapest and Prague tour. Why?

1. They know this tour. They can, with enthusiasm, knowledge, and conviction, tell others about it.

2. Aim to get fifteen people to come on next year's tour. (Or have a separate tour led by Adam and/or Gabriela.) Then they could come free, or go on another tour free.

3. Also it is good sales training. They "know the product," and are enthusiastic about it.

Is this the beginning of a JGI franchise? A tour franchise? Should I study franchises? I'd like to learn something new.

Sales Dynamism!

I started out this morning with a very concrete idea.

Goal: Get twenty-five people for next year's Budapest and Prague tour.

Aim for twenty-five. Start collecting names and deposits now.

I have to get people to register for my tours. That is a and the bottom line. This dynamic approach focuses me on actual people! Its dynamism centers me!

This constant sales dynamism could flood my daily life. Is it the motivating tool beyond fear I have been looking for. It all feels right.

Focusing on others through constant sales dynamism. Flood my being down to its roots.

I am introducing a new word into my lexicon: dynamism.

It symbolizes a new life style and concept as well.

Unleashed Life is the title of this *New Leaf*. Constant sales dynamism welds art to business. It combines artistic energies with going public. Dynamism signifies unleashed life and unleashed passion at its best.

It Only Took Thirty-Five Years

This constant sales dynamism solves my money problem because it resolves my conflict between art and business.

Wouldn't it be strange, if all along, I never really had a money problem. My so-called money problem really masked my conflict between art and business. My constant fear of poverty was really a fear that I would "have to work" meaning, get a regular job, and thus give up my artistic life. I would have to sacrifice the beautiful inner chamber of my imagination, trade it in to "make a living." Ugh, ugh, and triple ugh! How I absolutely hate that thought! Never, never, never! That was my only answer. Yet the fear of "slipping back" into "making a living" through a lifeless, boring job, killing all my artistic desires and my beautiful imagination along with it, always hovered in the back of my mind.

It took the form of money worries. These worries started in earnest when I got married and had to support a family. It just intensifies my artistic/business conflict.

That conflict has been resolved. And it only took thirty-five years!

Great Sales Campaign of 2003

Lubrication factor: I like that word combo. I means preparing and moving forward. I'm lubricating mind and fingers, waiting for something to happen. When it does, I'll be ready.

What can possibly happen? Well, a good streak of writing could jump upon me, or a good idea could pop up during the writing process. Or, nothing might happen. That in itself would be okay, too because writing about nothing is part of the lubrication process.

Anyway, here I am today, sitting and spewing. Words going ding dong across the pages.

In the lubrication process, I prepare for the Great Sales Campaign of 2003. A devotion well spent.

The Great Sales Campaign of 2003 is actually a religious event. An epiphany. Aha, strong stuff. I sneeze my way to Orion. Religious event. Epiphany. This definitely raises sales to a higher level. Indeed, the highest! Sales as a spiritual event, sales as high sneezing form, sales as a blowout dedication to the Lord of Vibrations above. Humble sales, which used to crawl with the snails at the bottom of the earth has been raised higher than a church spire. Reaching even higher, higher than a spire. . . upward, upward. . . to in-spire. Inspiration breathing fire, sales as the dynamic dualism, an agricultural monster welding corn cobs and steeples together, blending the vibrations of earthly vicissitudes with the celestial planks of basement foundational fortitude.

Who would think Sales would rise so high or that they would ever warrant a capital letter. But indeed, that is what is pouring through my fingers this morning. Yes, the Sales-I has not only been resurrected, but it has taken off all its clothing, popping beyond all psychological expectations, rising to a cosmic and spiritual pinnacle. Mount Sinai Moses, my spiritual father, would be proud.

Explaining my Prices

Instead of being angry at people who complain about my tour or other prices being too "high," I would do better to "understand" it from their point of view. After all, if I was the buyer and paying, I would like to know why the reason for the price, why it is so "high;" I'd like to know "what I am paying for."

How to "explain" my price to people?: The answer is to "teach them," tell them about the quality of the tour, service, or article.

Yes, I want to explain my prices. It gives me a chance to talk about the tour, the intensity of its learning experience, the high quality of its leaders, personalized services, itinerary, and more.

This is also a good approach in explaining my prices for bookings, and weekends. Are they an excellent value!

There's a description: Excellent value.

My tours and bookings are excellent values. Look what you get for the price! Explain it.

Let me tell you what you get in this tour.

Let me tell you what you get when you hire me to lead folk dancing, play guitar, or both, for your event. I'll explain it.

See their opposition as a hidden sign of interest.

Love their resistence. Take it as an opportunity to explain.

Instead of defending my prices, I will go on the offensive. Dive right into the price itself. Explain it, even in detail. Show why and how their purchase is such an excellent value.

Money and prices strike directly at the heart.

This whole concept of prices and their explanation it is actually quite exciting. In fact, I can't wait to find a client, a potential customer, and start explaining. Let me at 'em! The tiger is hungry for red meat!

Yesterday morning I called all my E-mail people, made a list of folk dancer E-mail address (the ones I could find). It took about two hours of straight calling. In the evening, I group E-mail my schedule and Norwegian itinerary to the Florida Folk Dancers and the Folk Dance Network. A big day of E-mailing. Plus I'm almost finished with my ITN ad.

All in all, I've entered more fully into the technological age. Result of all yesterday's work: A sense of satisfaction. It feel good, real good! I like all this "in the world" sales and gospel working.

Is there excitement in this gone-public sales work? Yes. But the main feeling is one of inner peace and "technological" satisfaction.

Word of Mouth

It is much more interesting looking at an individual as hidden leader type than a isolated individual. The concept of hidden leader opens up and reveals their (obviously hidden) potential. Also it spreads the "word of mouth" idea.

Getting mouths to move; the mouth being closely related to brain, and one of the best, quickest pathways to the heart.

Word of mouth is the best advertising. My goal is to get the flow going, the flowing words from the mouth. From my mouth to their mouths.

That's why it is so important that I call them, talk to them, be there in their presence to create personal energy, mostly expressed through the mouth. Get the mouths to move, all the mouths of my customers and clients, dancers and travelers, business acquaintances and friends, all of them.

By seeing individuals as hidden leaders, I not only recognize and promote their potential but can also use them for my own purposes accordingly. They can both help themselves (by realizing and expanding their potential) and help me (by using their potential, power, friends, and word of mouth) to sales of my wonderful products and services, a win-win situation.

"Hire" all my clients and customers as sales people. Find the center of their enthusiasm; plug into it; use their (hidden) potential to increase my and "their" sales. It's an us-us situation.

Love and Care of Customers

There is another element emerging here: love and care for my customers. I love them, and I love caring for them.

Where do imagination, dreams, mysticism, and passion fit into this love? To find the answer, start with passion. Isn't passion part of love? Or love itself?

Dare I love my customers?

Use all my skills and talents in the service of love and serving others. Not a bad way to go.

Sales are my form of going-public love.

Attach a sales attitude to each phone call.

Say Hello, Then Go Right Past

What do you do about complaints of bitter, negative people? Try to convince them they are wrong? Try to change their opinions?

No. Best is to go right past them.

Be polite. Recognize them, say hello. Then go right past them.

Deal with my body complaints, its aches and pains, in the same manner: Recognize them, say hello. Then go right past them.

A Plus Side for the Nay Sayers

Nay sayers throw in the negative slant first. They are right. . .partly.

But their emphasis is on the negative. By interpreting the world through worry, they put fear before hope. Thus are their views "unbalanced."

Thank God for Nervousness!

All this work! I'm nervous about it. Trip to Santa Fe, upcoming Thursday-to-Saturday Folk Dance Weekend, Saturday night booking in Harriman, then the Staten Island bar mitzvah on Sunday.

So much work! Will I be able to do it?

I'm nervous. But I'm glad I'm nervous. Look how miserable I am when I'm not nervous. "Nervous" is my energy speaking. It's saying, get ready, rise up, prepare for your next challenge. It is stimulating, aggressive, and high. I love my nervousness! Thank God I have something to look forward to, be nervous about! I have an "excuse" to call up my energy and rise above myself.

Will focus on nervous energy cure my body pains? Yes.

Use it. . . and bless it!

That is why it is important to center my mind on the outside world of sales, business, and performance.

Such focus on public functioning makes me nervous. Nervous energy cures my woes.

Sales Are Performance!

Performance is in the outside world. It includes all areas of "outside my room" functioning, and the business world with its emphasis on sales.

Sales is a performance, a concert, folk dance teaching, and tour leading. Here all these forms meet.

This is so good for me!

Why? Performance makes me nervous. This nervousness can cure physical and mental aches and pains.

How? By focusing on performance.

The more I turn my energies towards performance in the outside world, the more I cure myself.

Practicing Sales Passion

The bookstore near the square in Santa Fe wouldn't buy my *New Leaf 1* or *2*. They sent me to the Ark Bookstore. The Ark bought both *Leaves*.

I felt old fears of rejection when I tried selling my books. But I went anyway because Sales are Important.

Nervousness before sales, fear of rejection, touched my energy center. It put me in touch with my powers.

That energy is a form of passion.

Thus book sales, like all other sales, are a form of passion. Sales as Passion! I like it.

But if sales are passion, they belong in Miracle Schedule.

Business has two aspects: Organization and Sales.

I organize a tour, then I sell it; I organize a concerts, folk dance classes, weekends, write a book, then sell them.

God organized the world by creating it. Organizing is creating. Thus, as creative act, organizing belongs on the miracle schedule.

If this is so, how about sales? Aren't sales creative acts? Maybe I haven't seen them this way in the past because sales contain fear, the fear of rejection.

There is little fear in organizing, creating, preparing, and writing. These take place in the safe chamber of my mind where they have yet to go public.

Bringing creations public carries them to fear's door. Fear of rejection prevented me from seeing sales as creative. But that does not mean sales are not creative; it only means I fear sales. Thus fear is an important aspect of the creative process.

Sales belong to Passion!

To practice this truth, start with the sale of *New Leaf.*

The Sales Center

When selling focus on the passion (nervous) energy it engenders and not on the sale itself. This kind of focus keeps you centered. It also takes you beyond the fear of rejection.

Focus on this Center can be applied to all other creative and artistic endeavors: guitar playing, folk dancing, and tours.

I need connection to others to make myself whole.

Sales are my people connection. They unify my many selves and make me whole.

Divinity in Tour Leadership

Is there divinity in tour leadership?

Well, why not?

If political leaders are (often quite subtly) connected to the divine, why not leaders in general? Why not folk dance or tour leaders? Why not me?

This certainly is an inspiring way to look at tours and tourism. It would place my role in a new light as well as give a healthy, needed "divine lift" to my concept of tour leadership, and my tour business.

There is divinity in leadership, any and all kinds of leadership. The ability to lead is a gift, a talent. Such an ability derives from higher consciousness and ultimately, from the Highest Consciousness.

Now the quest is how to stay in touch with this divinity as much as possible. . . ever hoping for permanent contact and connection.

Divinity is present and appears in a concert performance, reading, folk dance leading, tour leadership, event organizing (pre-leadership) and more.

It appears in private life. . . only less strongly. Private life with its private practice is really a preparation for public life with its public practice. The public has more energy vibrations thus gives the possibility for a more energetic connection with divinity. Look at the energy an audience contains; each audience member in it is a packet of vibrating molecules and energy emanation.

Do I Have the Dream?

My inability to build Jim Gold International into a large, multifaceted company with folk dance franchises, international tours, weekends, book sales, and guitar performances is one of my great failures.

I've survived as an entrepreneur but I have not thrived. I wonder why.

Is it something about my character? Or my deepest wishes? Is it that, deep down, I do not want such an organization? Or did I want it but was unable to find a market? Was I in the wrong place at the wrong time?

Well, "blaming" outside circumstances will never get me anywhere. The main question is: What do I really want?

Is it to be a writer, an artist?

Or is it to become an entrepreneur?

Or could I do both?

Well, I've done both, but the entrepreneur part has definitely suffered, taken a back seat, to the artist part.

What does all this have to do with dreams?

Here's a great quote I heard on the radio last night. A truck driver who built a billion dollar enterprise said, "If the dream is big enough, the facts don't count."

I love that one!

Certainly, my dream to become an artist was big enough. And I succeeded.

Was my dream to become an entrepreneur big enough?

Maybe not.

But I am at a new stage in life. I've succeeded in becoming an artist. Do I now have the interest, drive, dream to become an entrepreneur, to push the beautiful products and services I have developed?

Do I have the personality to become this kind of entrepreneur? Do I have the ability?

I do.

Thus the real question is: Do I have the interest? And the motivation?

Well, if I have the interest, I have the motivation.

Am I ready, willing, and desirous of now taking on the world, of becoming "that entrepreneur?"

I don't know.

I love being an artist. The entrepreneur part is something I have learned to do in order to survive. It is a necessary but secondary annoyance, an adjunct to the central artistic pillar.

Is this the reason I have not "succeeded" in it?

Probably.

An aspect of myself likes going public. It likes the social give and take of working with audiences. This is my entrepreneurial self on display.

Showing myself and my wares: How much time and effort does my inner self want to put into this? If I subtract the nice and necessary aspect of money and financial security, how much of inner me is really interested? If I had all my wishes, wouldn't I rather play guitar or play in the park? Isn't it more fun to squirt water at the fountain and dream great dreams?

1. Is it more fun to dream great dreams than to realize them?

2. Yet I do need the outside world to push me beyond myself.

First is the artistic self; second is the entrepreneurial self.

I really need both. With only dreams, I would sink into myself, lose energy, and get depressed. With only my entrepreneurial self pushing, I would lose track of my inner source, forget my center, lose energy, feel hollow, and also get depressed.

I must create my art, then push and promote it. The latter in itself is a learning process. Thus only a combination of artist/entrepreneur is satisfactory.

So where am I? What about a new beginning for post-transitional me?

Somehow the entrepreneurial me has to touch my artistic center. They must fuse. Entrepreneur and artist must become one.

This is my present quest.

Is a there a way of approaching entrepreneurship as a student? Or, am I once again trying to find another way of avoiding the pain of (sales) rejection?

Money!

I know I can make money as an artist! I have full belief and confidence. I also know I can make more money as an artist than in the stock market.

As an artist, what skills and talents can I use to make money?

1. Artistic sales skills: I am an artist on the phone and with people.

2. Artistic products. All products Jim Gold International sells are artistic products. These consist of tours, weekends, folk dance classes, guitar and song concerts, booking, and my books. Promoting and selling these can be an incredible way of making money! By putting all of my efforts into selling and promoting what I already do and have done, I can make mucho. It would dwarf any stock market earnings

Could I earn an extra $40,000 this year in my business? Why not?

How? Through tours and bookings, of course. With some folk dancing on the side for daily expenses. Also the folk dance base does feed the tours. . . and a few bookings, too. Nevertheless, my main emphasis must be on tours and bookings.

This means advertising, mailings, and mucho sales calls. We know I am good at this stuff. Now it a matter of doing it.

We can keep the stock market interest bouncing on the side. Most of my learning in it has been done. The art of stop-loss is the main learning.

This is a new year, a post-transformational Icelandic year. Spend it promoting and pushing my tour and booking businesses.

God and Business (Continued): Business is Fun!

If business, in the personalized form of JGI, subsumes the miracle schedule, then doing business fills in all the empty spaces, connects all the dots. Business with its the God attachment, Business with its big "B," completes my world.

I came to this amazing realization in Greece, home of Western civilization, values, and culture.

All-Is-One is completed when dark and dirty worlds of capitalism and business, accompanied and guided by heir artistic angels and entrepreneurial shepherds, rush into the light.

Added to this is the holy idea that Business is Fun!

Why holy? The Psalms say worship God with joy, *b'simcha*.

Fun is joy differently spelled.

Would this mean that when you have fun you are worshiping God? Probably.

Fun is deeply related to joy. It is joy "lite." Since we are imperfect and worship imperfectly, I can even say fun and joy are the same! Imperfectly the same.

I am onto a deep personal truth. My personal skills and talents: leadership, diplomacy, handling and dealing with others, easy manner, organizational abilities, drive to get it right, and love of mitzvahs all come together in the fun world of Business.

"Nothing Better To Do". . . Shaking Hands with God

Woke up with a headache this morning. I have "nothing better to do" than go on this morning's bus tour.

Nothing better to do! Imagine that. No writing, running, reading, studying. . . . I have nothing better to do than be with my guests, my customers, my clients.

I'm not even practicing my Greek. All of my mind is on running this tour as well as I can, focusing on the needs, happiness, and satisfaction of my customers. All other areas have been cleared.

Wouldn't I like to find a "higher" interest? But perhaps focusing on my customers, putting myself in the service of others, is a higher interest. It might even the highest interest. And, as such, be part of the fun, the joy, the worship of God.

Serve God with joy.

Truly, it is mucho fun focusing on the attempt to satisfy the needs of others. Helping them is a mitzvah that brings me great satisfaction.

So what does "nothing better to do" mean? Perhaps, deep within the psychic nothingness, the Buddhist void, stands the Lord Himself.

This turns "nothing" into Everything.

I serve myself best when I serve others.

By serving others, I best serve myself.

How?

By surmounting ego, bypassing the little self, moving straight into the customer-focus land of Universal Big Self Me.

Rather than lost, I am found! This new feeling takes some getting used to.

Perhaps this morning's headache comes not from anger or annoyance but rather a suppression of joy!

This makes sense. It has been an excellent and glorious tour. I have run it beautifully. With all my skills and instincts working full time, I moved straight on and straight ahead. Going to the Plaka with my group and staying with them despite my fatigue was a gut level and instinctual Yes! I did the right thing.

By going on this morning's city tour, accompanying and escorting my clients, being at their side, I again did the right thing.

Doing the right thing brought me joy! In this worshiping process, I shake hands with God.

Indeed, it is a joy headache.

Denying my own joy is a denial of the higher forces.

Face the light: Learn to love it!

Bills as Payments. . . to Myself!

Hiring Myra, and paying her $200 a month to sell and promote tours is really a form of paying myself to think harder.

Paying bills of any kind is a form of paying oneself.

What an excellent way of seeing bills. . . as forms of payment to myself!

This kind of philosophy certainly cuts down on bill resentment. It might even help me appreciate what I'm paying for. Someday I might even learn to enjoy paying bills!

I am at an Ending.
I Can't Wait for my Next Beginning!
I finished recording all of my dances. A major fist step has been completed.
What is next? I always need a direction.
It may be a week of rest and recovery. Recovery could last hours, days, or even weeks, maybe six weeks. During that time a new energy system may emerge.
Take a break, read.
So-called "rest and recovery" is an uncomfortable place.
I don't like it. I like direction filled with energy.
I am at an ending.
I can't wait for my next beginning!

Work Like Crazy!

First, I finished recording all my dances into computer files. Then, last night, I finished burning the entire collection of my folk dance files onto CD's. Hour after hour, I blazed them out, one after another
It is a real high for me to work like crazy!
What should I do with the emptiness that follows completion?
Evidently, I need to fill it with a new project that will spur me on.
The new and future project might be. . . recording! Learning how to record my guitar and songs; then put myself into my computer's music files!

My First Sales Performance

I just gave my first Sales Performance in the kitchen. I followed my natural instincts. Here's how it went:
First I played "St. Louis Tickle." Very slowly in warm up mode.

Verdict on my playing: Passable but slow.

Second came "Alhambra". Mostly the bass came out. Treble stiff and almost non-existent. Verdict: passable but with demonstrably weak, "unwarmed up" tremolo.

Then I felt so tired, I gave up playing, put down my guitar, lay down in bed and went to sleep.

Idea: Suppose I gave a sales performance, and, after playing "St. Louis Tickle" and "Alhambra," instead of putting down my guitar, laying down in bed, and going to sleep, I told the audience I felt tired, put down my guitar, and went to sleep right on stage! Wouldn't that be a reality sales performance? Wouldn't that be a manifestation of the real me living in the reality of the moment?

Why not give it a try? What do I have to lose but my dignity and business?

Would my audience be interested in such a real me? If I demonstrated such a real me, would it be a sales performance or a sales close out?

My Byzantine Empire

Use the Byzantine Empire as a model.

Disparate parts weld into one.

Playing guitar is an expression, extension, and expansion of the Byzantine JGI empire. So are all the other "themes."

Proper administration of my empire is the next challenge.

Sales is brute work only when I see it in the narrow sense of selling one particular product, one aspect of the miracle schedule, one member of the JGI empire, that it becomes oppressive. It is not sales itself that bother me. Rather it is the narrowness of my vision.

But when I see sales as an expression, extension, and expansion of the whole JGI Miracle Schedule Empire, and an important part of its administration, then it takes on an entirely different meaning.

Administration is a new word in my *New Leaf* vocabulary.

I am at the edge of bringing administration, history, and politics together in a new and personal JGI Empire web. A coalition and a coalescing.

A president sells his administration to the public by explaining it.

Thus he promotes his agenda.

I can sell my JGI administration to the public by explaining its purpose, goal, and meaning.

The Artistic Oneness and Unity of Sales

Money is people spelt differently.

I need money. I am dependent upon getting it. But I need people even more. I am totally dependent upon them.

Knowing the pain and beauty of this spiritual truth is my key to wholeness of sales.

Sales Are Just Plain Fun!

Sales are just plain fun!

What a statement for me to make!

Organizing tours, too: Just plain fun! Even dealing with Bill's organizational and financial screw-ups, and trying to figure things out, is fun.

I approach a new level of fun. This one is based on dealing with earthly reality! No separation between business and art. I weld spiritual, mental, and material realities together in one growth-and-excitement, energy-filled, inspired and loving moment.

The fruit has ripened and fallen from the tree. Amazing!

Mad Shoe Salesman!

I always wanted to run wild on the lawn.

Could I have always, secretly been, a running-wild-on-the-lawn, mad shoe salesman?

That shoe salesman is the biggest secret I have kept, not only from others, but from myself.

Is stage fright a form of sales fright? Is it caused by fear of mad shoe sales energy?

I know and grew up with many people who were in small businesses (entrepreneurs). As a dentist, my uncle Willie was in the small business. My private violin teachers, Vladimir Grafman, Sam Furman, my piano teacher, Mrs. Weissbarth, all were in their own business. Today, private teachers, professionals etc. are all in their own business. Even my wife is in her own business!

Members of the music profession, for some reason, do not consider themselves to be businessmen or entrepreneurs. They are, instead, "professionals. . . whatever that means. Maybe it is even a way of snobbishly putting themselves above small business, above the fray, somehow making themselves more important. But seeing it this way may be a result of my own prejudice. After all, I grew up looking down on the businessman, the capitalist, and money making in general. Mine was the communist, others, and the government will, and should, take care of you.

The dentist, private psychiatric practitioner, private teacher, all belong in the entrepreneurial category. And this whether they see it that way or not.

The only advantage they may have is selling their skills may be less risky than artists trying to sell their creations. There may simply be more of a market for them.

Tour Deepening

The First Step in-Depth Tour Direction Step

We're in Ljubljana. Our new guide, Blaz Bostjancic, is a winner. Last night, after a beautiful gourmet supper at the Union Hotel, we spoke about a future May, 2006 tour: It would include three or four days in Germany (Bavaria: Munich, Salzburg, or both), three or four days in northern Italy (the Trieste region, Venezia Julia), and one week in Slovenia. This would mean three countries: Germany, Italy, Slovenia, and three languages: German, Italian, Slovenian, three linguistic branches: Germanic, Latin, and Slavic. It would also include yodeling, lederhosen, and folklore festivals in, say, Maribor, Tre Glav, etc.

I would be studying three new regions: Bavarian history (of which I know almost nothing), northern Italian history, Lombards, etc (of which I know almost nothing), and Slovenian history (of which I know almost nothing.) A winner!

Rebirth mode!

And I might still go to Japan!

A general explosion of self, expansion, and depth!

Let the *B'simcha* Flow

As I sit, at 4:30 p.m. on the fourth floor, Hotel Argentina restaurant overlooking Dubrovnik, its bay, and the Adriatic sea, I ask: "Am I somatizing my tour?"

I think I am.

The mental prison of our itinerary structure is being expressed through my body. I feel caught, trapped in tour tensions.

Why do I do this to myself?

In some strange, twisted, masochistic sense, I must feel these aches and pains are "good" for me. Somehow they protect me.

Against what?

Perhaps the randomness quality of touring, its lack of structure, coupled with the constant threat of falling into an abyss of disorganization with its black hole of chaos.

Left knee, left inner thigh, left shoulder pain, back pain, and a few others. . . . .

Do I still need these pains?

Also, for some reason, I "refuse" to exercise. I fear that if I dissolve my pains through yoga and calliyoga, I'll forget about my tour. The pain reminds me I am working. It somehow keeps me focused on my responsibilities as leader. I cannot allow myself to heal until the tour is over.

Is there another way to think? Can I eliminate pain and run my tour?

Do these physical sufferings belong to the old neighborhood? Are they a residue of my former confidence lacking leadership?

But I am now living in a post-transitional place. Here, theoretically, I do not "need" my old pains.

Can I keep my total focus and still run a tour without pain? Indeed, such an attitude would express a new simcha self.

Vibrate with *Simcha* Joy

I feel bad because I now like Harold. I enjoyed feeling both he and his wife were difficult, complaining tourists (but enthusiastic too.) But now, since he sincerely said he is concerned about my feelings, I want to like him more. And perhaps I do. Nevertheless, I so enjoyed my annoyance at their complaining. Somehow it energized me. . . in an old neighborhood way.

I'm also annoyed because we must see the Hungarian State Ensemble tonight. This instead of having a night off. The whole group wants to go so I feel it is my duty, responsibility, and obligation to go with them even though no one "expects" me to go. Yet, deep down, I know part of them does expect me to go. I am the leader. I should show up and be there. I both believe this and resent the obligation.

Well, what else would I do tonight? Stay home and watch TV? As long as I am with the group, I am not "free." That is the annoyance. But it is also the glory! When I am with them I still play my role; when I work I can still be a hero. And isn't that what I really want?

Yes, I want to be my own hero. In the process, I might also become other people's hero, a hero to my group. Some of them may believe that even now. But most important is that I be a hero to myself. Leading gives me another chance to be one.

How to become a hero? I don't have to do anything. But I do have to think a certain way. Think heroic thoughts. The most heroic thought for me as tour leader is enthusiasm, the spreading of simcha in my group. How do I do that? By projecting simcha vibrations. Projecting the positive while under pressure to perform in public is more difficult than quietly feeling them in private.

Yes, as my tourists negotiate their way through a foreign land, the presence of a tour leader makes them feel more secure. If I can add a touch of simcha, and then spread it around, that's even better.

Why then am I anxious for my tour responsibilities to end? Because I have forgotten my role and purpose not only on this tour, but in life. That purpose is to follow my passion, fly with enthusiasm, and let the wild simcha flow.

This is what I can give my tourists and myself.

Vibrate with simcha joy: That is the meditation I want to focus on and remember. What better place to practice than leading a tour.

Fulfillment

And the birth of Folk Festival Tours

The Folkloriada Tour of Hungary is just about over. Today we return to Budapest via Kalosca. Tomorrow we fly home.

The tour has been a big success on every level. I succeed in fulfilling my first pre-tour goal: Run the best tour possible with full focus and concentration. As for my second goal: Run it with God worshiping *b'simcha*, I was partially successful. *b'simcha* was scattered throughout much of the tour when ideas of resurrection and renaissance occurred. It took place more fully during the last few days, when I was finally able to relax, write, reflect, and run.

Indeed, I am returning to America reborn in almost every aspect of my miracle schedule. And this time, it includes business! Specifically, the tour business. (Terry's idea of specializing in festivals, Folk Festival Tours, is such a good one. See my hand-written notebook for details.)

The sadness of a tour ending can be softened with a *b'simcha* attitude. . .softened, but not eliminated.

But why eliminate it?

Sadness itself is part of *b'simcha*.

After all, don't we cry for joy?

Depression is part of *b'simcha* attitude? Why not?

Look at the sentence: "I'm so busy I'm not even giving myself the luxury of getting depressed. Here depression is seen as a subtle and hidden energizer. A positive in negative form.

Thus depression and sadness: both in subtle ways, belong to *b'simcha*.

What better way to express *b'simcha* than through a festival. Folk Festival Tours: A business expression of *b'simcha*.

A place where miracle schedule and business meet: The *b'simcha* place. A makom kadesh.

When I return home to bills, worries, problems, miseries, and the suffering I often call life, bring part of my tour with me. I'll take the worshipful practice of *b'simcha* attitude, not only in dance, but in everything I do.

As I sat in meditative yogic pose in the sculpture park, Jodi asked me, "Swami, what is the meaning of life?"

As that moment, the higher forces were not with me, so all I could think of saying was "Lunch is being served."

But this morning, I expanded this phrase beyond the material plane: "Celestial lunch is being served." On this Folkloriada Festival tour, we have been served celestial lunches, dance lunches, joyful food for the soul.

Folk Dance Resentment and Back Pain

The idea that I can start my sales project right now, a project I have been thinking about and mentally preparing for several months, makes me feel very good. I am ready to go despite lack of mailing, flier, and even prices.

Yes. it makes me feel very good. And this, in spite of the fact that my back is killing me! I haven't had such a back pain for years. What minor pain have come up, I've been easily able to handle. I take is a day or two off. Then, when the pain subsided, I glided back to my usual physical routines.

But now this back pain has absolutely crippled me. Daily, it seems to get worse, not better. And it has already lasted over three days. What is wrong? What would Dr. John Sarno say? What do I say?

Writing about all the possible psychological reason for this pain makes me feel better. Whether it helps my pain or not, I do not know. Well, perhaps it does. . . for awhile. Also, in the process of writing, I may be slowly curing myself. At least I hope this is true.

But somehow this pain is more intense than the rest, more painful, and more crippling.

Following the Dr. John Sarno rule and model, a good question to ask is: Why am I crippling myself? Why now?

Certainly, it has something to do with my post-tour down. It was a fabulous tour. I shone in all areas. The people loved it. I came out shocked full of new ideas.

If all these positives took place, why am I now crippling myself with untenable back pain?

Does it have something to do with returning to folk dancing? Do I resent returning to the folk dance field, putting all that time and effort into a field that pays so little (when tours can possibly pay so much)?

Is my back pain caused by folk dance resentment? Possibly.

I know I am screaming. . . with pain and anger. It could also be against returning to folk dancing.

Why?

I am returning to folk dancing un-reborn. Resurrection has flooded into the tour field and business. But it has not touched the folk dance field.

Is there a possible folk dance renaissance up ahead? Can I transfer my tour resurrection and rebirth to folk dancing? Now that I am back, is there any way of changing my approach. And if I do, will it cure my back pain?

Good questions, indeed.

How can I put new life into folk dancing?

Choreography seems to be the only answer. Create an entirely new repertoire. Labanotation is in sight; I could call it Jimanotation. Learn to labanotate, or at least Jimanotate. Write down my dances.

Choreography is creative. Do I want to return to the artistic creative life? Or would I rather make money?

The tour business symbolizes, among other things, the possiblity of making money, mucho money.

Should I drop folk dance teaching? Cut back my classes? Are they worth it? What questions!

Artist Unites All

By nature, I am an artist. But, during the past twenty-five years I have also wanted to become a businessman and a CEO. Deep down I may never have wanted to. But I was tired of constantly being afraid of having no money. I wanted a better way of dealing with the outside, material world. . . so that I could eventually go back to being my true self: an artist.

Well, the financial route was twisted, long, and destructive.

Mostly, it destroyed this concept of myself. Thank God for that! As I stand in the aftermath of this storm, I look around at the ashes upon which I shall build my new life. To artist I have added entrepreneur. As a Gemini, this dual definition of self fits. The artist/entrepreneurial path is the right one for me.

Margining, borrowing money, and learning to play the stock market was a mistaken path. But evidently, I had to take it to find this out. Again, as Emmanuel said, now that I have learned my lesson, the illness will go away.

Can one be a passionate businessman? Can artist and entrepreneur be combined? Can both flourish under the rubric of Passion? I also have organizational and leadership skills. Where do they come in? Rajasic, tamasic, or sattvic?

"Tamasic qualities are selfish and inert. Sattvic qualities are harmonious, balanced, and tranquil-minded. Rajasic is dynam

Organizational and leadership talents are definitely not tamasic, not selfish and inert. They are partly rajasic. But they may be sattvic. Organization and leadership (inspiring others to follow your the dreams and visions behind your organizing principle, your "organization," certainly create or put one on the trail of harmony, balance, and ultimately, tranquility of mind.

Therefore, my tour business, my entrepreneurial bent, could have a sattvic quality. And, being a Gemini whose key word is "both," (or even "many"), combining rajasic and sattvic would feel right and reasonable.

I am not, cannot be, will never be, a "businessman." For me, there can be no such rational, abstract thing. I can no longer call mine a "tour business, folk dance business, weekend business, booking business, guitar concert business, writing business."

Business is a reflection of raja, passion, and the artistic soul. *b'simcha* will come from focus on and remembrance of this truth.

Ideas of building an organization and giving a house concert came to me simultaneously. They are twins and thus as developments, somehow related. But I don't know how yet.

Of course, concerts are a way of spreading the word, and finding new and more people to build an organization. But although true, these are old thoughts, old ways of thinking.

Let the whole thing marinate. See where it leads.

Rolling Along Sales: I Love It!

I am entering a brand new place: The land of The Great Playpen where rolling along sales, and scintillating, out-there, gone public, excitement reigns.

Everything is falling together in one great organizational whole. It feels even more exciting than the individual spokes of the JGI wheel, the individual tours, weekends, folk dance classes, bookings, book sales, and more. A great sizzling, wind-blown, sales, out-there, gone public whole.

It is One Volcano erupting with One Lava Flow rolling down the mountains and flooding the valleys.

There is nothing else to do but this, nowhere else to go, nowhere else to be but here.

Everything feels in order, in place; I am in a scintillating and sizzling. I am here. Or am I there? Here, there, where ever here or there is, I am in it.

Is this place really so "new?" I think so.

The Great Playpen of outdoors meets the immature, artistic, in-room Mind. And they embrace!

It's so much fun I can hardly stand it!

I am entering a new land with new vistas.

Competition

Competition versus planning is similar to spontaneity versus organization. One can either be spontaneous or organized (planned), but one cannot be both. When one tries to be, both forces are vitiated; and an inferior product results.

I fall flat on the side of individual creativity. Sure I need planning, but I want to plan my own. When I look around at my competitors, their strengths will help me plan and freely make a decision of what is best to do.

True, I have always hated my competition and wanted to destroy it. Competitors whether they are Karl Finger, Andres Segovia, or my little sister in childhood, always make me feel somewhat diminished and awful. Yet I also realize that, without them, there would be no folk dance, guitar, or other field for me. Their existence also gives me ideas and directions for which way to go. Although I hate them, I also need them. Deep down I even love them.

I have always been too jealous and envious of my competitors to look at the influence of their competition upon me. Competition, entrepreneurism, and capitalism are triplets.

Competition touches that feeling of grit and dynamism in my stomach. It dumps my solar plexus energy into the market place.

It grounds me in the dynamism of material and economic reality.

Should I compete with death?
Yes!

I have usually denied the effects of competition, denied that I even compete or have any competitors. I try to stay in my own entrepreneurial world because it is just too painful to look the fact that an outside competition actually exists.

Does this painful view of competition stem from competing with my twin sister at an early age? Does it comes from being brought up a communist, learning to hate the capitalist, competitive society? Both?

One thing I can see is that merely looking at the issue activates the energy enzymes in my stomach; it wakes me up and focuses me.

There must be something good in this new solar plexus, energy arousal, this competitive wake up call.

Wrestling with the Sales Monster

This morning, I awoke a 4:30 a.m. with a vision. I saw a Pastel of People. Each person was a spark.

I felt a sudden whiff of fresh air. That's a start.

From that start I'll reinvigorate my activities. How that will be done, I do not know. So, I'll keep rambling on until I find out.

The "pastel of people vision" means I will be building contacts and customers, a tour business, not just for this year's tour, but for future tours as well. Thus if I consider tours to Romania, and Serbia, even Austria and Slovenia (and Northern Italy) for 2006 (and perhaps Adam's Pepper Festival Hungary tour), I'd be finding customers for them.

I'll be expanding, reaching out, experimenting and searching out new sales techniques.

My whole "new" world, is now centered on (the formerly hated) sales. Reaching out for new customers and business, building an organization based on a pastel of people. No matter how I phrase it, even using the artistic "Pastel of People vision," it all boils down again to sales.

Old questions return: Could sales ever excite me? Would my former communist self with my communist mother leaning over me, ever allow myself to become excited about sales?

Perhaps wrestling with this question is what is killing my enthusiasm. After all, how could this former communist admit that sales, a check in the mail, a registration, money itself, could inspire and excite me. And this, even though there is no question that it does.

Is my down, the last three-month killing of my enthusiasm, once again due to the return of this life time question? Is it really so "simple?"

Truly there is nothing left for me to do but sell. I've done everything else. Been everywhere, done that. Succeeded in everything. . .but sales.

And this even though I am good at it. I'm a "natural" salesman.

Is it time to face this "fact?" Is the denial of this monster killing my enthusiasm?

Is the only study left to me, the study of sales, sales technique and sales technique improvement?

I like improvement. I like to grow. I need to as well.

But in the (ugh) sales direction?

Notice the "ugh" is still there. I have yet to change, to transform this vital substratum of my personality. Will I ever? Do I even have a choice? If I don't transform myself, I will be doomed to an passionless, unenthusiastic existence.

It is time to wrestle with the sales monster.

I am at the point where sales is the only thing I can do, the only thing I am "interested" in doing. Indeed, I am wrestling with the big one.

As for study, for inspiration, direction, re-education, and enthusiasm, I might look into the lives of the great entrepreneurs, salesmen, and capitalists.

I might also say that this sales monster has always been the big block in my life. My oppositional and anti-sales attitude has always been my prime obstacle to making money and business growth.

Perhaps I am now ready to face and deal with this biggest, this greatest of challenges. I hope so. I know there is nothing else left for me to do. For me it is now the marketing, sales, and business growth direction. . . or die.

How do I do this? Where do I start?

A first step might be to transform my miracle schedule into a "sales schedule." Funnel the "miracle activities" into an outward, public, gone-public, pastel of people, organizational, marketing, and sales direction.

How?

How do I turn yoga into sales? What is a sales push-up? Etc.

My attitude has to change, be redirected, and reorganized.

Aches and pains, in order to have meaning, now have to become sales aches and pains.

Linguistic study has to be refocused. Sell foreign words. This can be done only by going on tour.

Total Sales Involvement Express "Pastel of People"

Sick with a bad cold. Slept nine hours.

Let's face it: There is nothing I want to do or focus on now except call, make sales call, organize my pastel of people! Nothing in or of my miracle schedule works anymore. I'm at the end of it. If it is to survive, it will need a new form.

I repeat: Focus is now totally on making sales calls and deeply organizing my Pastel of People.

This alone can be considered a strange victory. I've never, deeply in my soul, wanted to promote, sell, and organize. It is, or at least feels like, a new kind of wanting (whatever that means.)

Well, for whatever reason it is occurring, this total wanting to make sales calls and organize my pastel of peoples, this "new wanting" is where I am. Accept it, and deal with it.

First, comes the dropping of all former miracle schedule deeds and approaches. This will make room for a new, "fresh, young wanting."

Second, use the new wanting to energize myself. In the process, cure my present cold and left shoulder pain.

Somehow (now I am improvising) the energy and freshness from the new wanting will have to flow into and revitalize my miracle schedule, not vice versa. Public will now be revitalizing private, rather than the other way around. In other words, my whole psyche has been reversed and now stands on its head.

With Relish!

Is it a realistic crashing down, or realistic crashing up?

Helen is the Slovak tour woman from Rochester, New York who said, "Jim, rather than limit your tour to thirty, thirty-five, forty, or whatever, let it expand to whatever God wants. Let God decide on the numbers. You just fill the orders and do your work." Thus she gave me the idea of accepting and taking anyone and everyone who registers for my Bulgarian tour.

After I told Carol about the Helen idea and our November, 2005 Woodstock Artist and Folk Dance, and that I was limiting it to forty people, she asked: "Why? Why not open it up anyone and everyone like the Bulgarian? As for the Artist Studio visits, you can do them in shifts. Supper in the restaurants too."

I said, "Wow! Why not? What a concept. My challenge then would become, not can I handle the flow, but can I handle the flood? This, of course, if we do have such a large, nay massive registration. But, of course, whether we do or don't is up to God. I at least can mentally prepare for the possibility of such numbers. In fact, by mentally imaging them, thinking about them, picturing them in my mind, I may even create the mental (and spiritual) energy for them to happen. After all, God an I work together. If I do my job, He'll do His. My only control is over my effort. Results are up to Him.

Elana is a former Israeli dancer who married a Mexican (thus her last name), and now lives in California. I have never met her. She was the first one to register for next year's Bulgarian tour. Elana sounds Israeli-sabra tough, pushy, and interesting. She called last night and woke me from a deep, cold-recovering sleep. "Did you get my E-mail?" she asked. I answered, "No" in my sleepy, throaty, cold-filled, snot-congested voice. "I need to know some things," she continued. "What are the exact Bulgarian tour dates, what flight and flight number are you taking, what is its time of arrival in Sofia, what is the exact address of the Radisson Hotel? I'm doing Land Only and am making my own flight arrangements from California."

Sleepily, I went to my den, booted up my computer, and opened my Bulgarian folder to find I had no written flight information or confirmation from Paul Laifer. I'll have to call him today to find out.

I told Elana I would mail and E-mail all the information to her. But her call reminded me of all the details, possible slip-ups, and moment-to-moment decisions and problems I always face when running a tour. Her call brought me down to reality. That's why it made me feel a bit down.

But, of course, this morning's question is: "Is it a realistic crashing down to reality, or a realistic crashing up to reality?"

I choose the positive; I chose up.

I need a new challenge. The "having done it all" life of the past few months is quite boring, bordering on depressing. And this even though things are going quite well.

My attitude towards the problems Elana threw at me is: I am facing them with relish!

Yes, I have "nothing else to do," no other old miracle schedules challenges to face. Now facing and organizing the new reality is my next big challenge.

"Pastel of People" is a business vision par excellence. It is worth every shoulder pain!

It is based on the beautiful and poetic concept that reality is a dream, a hazy pastel painting. In this hard-edge world of material existence, few people may say or even believe that "La Vida es Sueno." But I have believed it all my life.

Crossing from Private Imagination to Public Creation

My imagination is working in public. My dreams are coming true. Travelers are registering for tours. Bookings are coming in; folk dancers are showing up. I'm cooking on all burners. I'm loving it! The pomegranate has burst, cornucopia is exploding. I'm pouring in all directions.

Certainly this is enthusiasm, excitement, and exuberance gone wild. And it's all gone public. I'm out there selling, promoting, and dancing with a vengeance.

Sales and promoting are forms of dancing with my mouth. If my mouth moves, can my brain be far behind?

My private dreams, created in the in-room of my imagination, are now, through the practical application of business and sales techniques, being recreated out there in public.

Yes, business and sales practice is my form of running wild in public. It's mad shoe mouth with mad mind brain following closely behind.

The bridge from private imagination to public creation has been crossed.

Turn My Ventures and Adventures into Art Forms

I read an article in the Wall Street Journal this morning entitled The Post-Saddam Boom. It said that investment in the Middle East has risen everywhere; in fact, it has leaped. (You'd never know about this optimism by reading the New York Times which is mostly full of gloom and doom about the present and future of the Middle East.)

In any case, what does this mean for me? It means that soon, eventually, perhaps even next year, I can start running tour to the Middle East again. I can start with Israel in spring of 2006. Then perhaps add Egypt, and even return to Tunisia. I can do Morocco.

And I always loved studying the Semitic languages, and especially writing in Arabic.

All this means returning to old forms, old places, old ideas. All were good to begin with. But I have to give them a new birth. One way would be to look at these ventures as art forms.

How to turn my ventures and adventures into art forms?

What are Folk Dances?

The new markets and new people concept also applies to the new Mario Battista Salsa Workshop I just booked for my Monday night folk dance group on March 21st. I'll promote it with the hope of attracting no only former folk dancers, but new dancers, new people as well. Maybe I can even expand my folk dance classes through some social dance workshops. Actually, salsa, rhumba, samba. meringue, mambo are not "social dances" (whatever that is) but Latin folk dances.

Is that true? In general, are so-called "social dances" really folk dances in disguise? Are the labels, "social" and "folk" really false distinctions? After all, "folk" do both kinds.

Dances: Are Salsa, Rhumba, Samba, Meringue, and Mambo really folk dances in disguise?

Tours: Will such an exploration and study eventually bring me run a tour to South America (or at least Dominican Republic) in order to learn more about these dance forms?

Wouldn't all this talk also be true for guitar playing? There are differences in styles, distinctions between forms; but ultimately, there is only One Guitar Playing. And this is done by people.

The Millionaire Goal

Why am I resurrecting the millionaire dream?

First of all, I like it. The vision energizes me.

How can I fulfill the millionaire vision? And this only through my business, my work, my personal efforts. The stock market and waiting for heaven to drop its bountiful gifts effortlessly into my lap is dead, gone, buried, over.

The millionaire vision is a mad vision. That's why I like it. "Madness has the advantage of surprise." A great "Yes!" to this John Batchelor line.

I Am a Salesman!

Well, Ma, I finally have a real job, a steady job, one that will make money. I am in promotion, publicity, and advertising. I'm a walking advertising agency. My job is to promote and sell. Yes, I am a salesman. Even though Arthur Miller's died, and Death of a Salesman Willie's died, and even though all communists think it is shameful, and also artists (I among them), in spite of all these negatives images, I finally am at the realization of my social, public, and ever personal self-image: I am a salesman.

That is my job. I have other skills. They are meaningful, too. Nevertheless, all my skill and talents would remain in the closet if not for my salesman work and identity.

On first glimpse, this is a crushing blow to my artistic image. What about my creative self? Where will it go? Probably nowhere. If I do not promote them, my arts will stay in the closet.

Evidently, it is personally very important to me that they do not stay in the closet. After their creation in the laboratory of mind and actual laboratory of my home, their next step, and the culmination of their existence, is to get them out of the house and into the public. The public may hate them, love them, ignore them, or who knows? Public opinions are beyond my control. But my job is to get them out there, to set my ships on the water.

I am a salesman. Promotion, advertising, and publicity are what I do. So did St. Paul. Gospel time is on hand.

I am not embracing the salesman life. It is more that I have no choice. That is the road right in front of my nose. My body aches as my mind changes its self-definition. I have always been a salesman!

Only I either didn't know it, or wouldn't face or admit it. Too shameful for an artist and communist. But those days are over.

A warm feeling of relaxation just came over me as I wrote those last lines.

Perhaps I can face, admit, come to peace with, and eventually even love my new salesman self.

Perhaps its warm flow will suffuse my body. That, indeed, would be its own kind of miracle.

Ready to Promote Folk Dancing

Next year will be a folk dance sales year. I will try to build up my folk dance classes. I see it as a three-year project.

Why am I doing this? It is not even for money. The money can be (although rarely is) found in the tour and booking business. Even guitar lessons yield more money than folk dance teaching. Yet I stay in it.

Aside from the fact that my folk dancers are part of my tour and weekend base, I also must admit: I thoroughly love it! I love the dances, the music, the people, the whole scenario of folk dancing in a circle together to beautiful music. When it works, it is sensational.

But, of course, the money has always been low to awful.

For some reason I can't or don't want to explain, I am ready to start promoting, selling, advertising, publicizing my folk dance teaching and folk dance classes. Maybe the reason is: I am just ready.

I see it as my long-term next project. I'm aiming to bring in the next generation. Naturally, as a side benefit, this will ultimately feed my weekends and tours. But this is not now my reason for doing it.

As I say, I am just ready.

A lover of private property, a lover of capitalism, a lover of business, a lover of the soul: Here is another reason why my back hurts. I may be inwardly furious that I am giving up my beautiful and fanciful life of the imagination, my creativity, in exchange for the "real" hard-edged practical world of business success.

Evidently, I must remain an artist first. Otherwise my back will really kill me.

The Advertising Self

How do I advertise my worthy wares? How do I let others know I exist? That is the heart of advertising.

It is the embryonic promotional me. I call it the advertising self.

Rather than develop new programs, my direction seems to be to promote and advertise the old ones. No new countries, weekends, or other. . .at least for now. Also no new miracle schedule aspects: no new yoga or running programs, or writing or guitar programs.

Rather promote, advertise. . .and even develop the old. Well, the development itself may be part of the promotion and advertising.

In any case, for now, for this year, for this period of personal development, advertising and promotion are the rule of the day.

That is why part of me feels I am "not moving." My programs are "standing still." Is this true? Well, yes and no. On the surface, they are not changing or moving. But perhaps internally, through their new advertising and promotional coloring, they are changing quite a bit. A new internal-external glow is developing within each program. They are now being fed and watered by "outside influences," namely, they are being fed by the great Gone-Public.

Where this will lead them, how this will change them, I do not yet know. But, no question, this new advertising and promotional approach is changing me. And as these subtle, internal changes take place within me, growth, development, and change also take place within my programs.

A good question, which I am not yet ready to answer, is, how will this new promotional and advertising attitude effect my yoga and running program? If a new self is doing yoga, if a new self is running, won't it be approaching and performing yoga and running in a new way? Same with guitar and writing.

No question this is all leading somewhere. But is may be still to early to tell exactly where.

Sell Them All!

Hard to believe, but I have finished ninety-eight per cent of my tour business sales! Here I thought March, April, and even parts of May would be mostly spent on the phone calling potential customers. Now, after about five weeks of intensive work, I've called almost everyone, put in all ads, and even E-mailed my entire list. I'm just about "finished." Amazing. There may be a few mop up sales things to do, and some cold e-mail sending to internet folk dance lists. But most of my tour sales work is done.

The sale of this year's tours has been so intense, I have just about forgotten everything else.

I have learned a great deal from the intensity of my personal sales involvement: mainly, I have learned that it works!

There is not a direct line between sales calls and actual sales. Sometimes, nay often, I call in one direction and the sales themselves come in another. I aim to the right, and sales come in from the left. Nevertheless, there is something magical about the vibrations of the sales energy I create when I make the effort. Somehow, when I put in the effort, actual sales occur. Sure, you have to go through yards of discouragement and frustration. But, in the end, if you add it all up, it works.

If it does in tours, would it not also work in other areas? Why not? How about books sales, CD sales, booking sales, concert sales, folk dance class sales, even Folk Dance Camp Weekend sales? All are part of my business. But I have not pursued them, put in the effort, because they do not pay as well as tours.

Now however, since my tour sales effort is slowing down, would it not be helpful, "educational," even inspiring to put my new sales attitude, skills, and desires into, say, selling my books?

Or how about a wider approach: Sell them all! All the step sisters. That means make the effort to sell not only books, but bookings, CD's, writings, folk dance classes, weekends, and, of course, more tours, too!

Great Business Idea: Uniting my Writing with Marketing

Dan Lampert's idea (and partly my own) of using my *New Leaf* writings for sales, advertising, and publicity is a wonderful one. "Take interesting quotes from my books and e-mail them to business leads every week." Then at the bottom of the page, put a convenient link to either/both "Update your mail profile at jimgold.com" or/and sign up for a Folk Tour."

Evidently, at this point, I will only be energized to act if there are (future and potential) sales involved—a self-energizing prospect. It may also explain why I can't put myself quite fully into language study, yoga, running, or any of my former miracle schedule activities. They are not (as yet) directly or even indirectly connected to future sales.

However, notice how writing and *New Leaf* can and will soon be connected! My writings will be used as sales tools in a newsletter type e-mail sales campaign. This may, some day be true for other miracles schedule activities. . . . but I don't see how. . . yet.

Writing is the first former in-room imagination, chamber of the mind, non-public miracle schedule bastion to "fall."

Writing goes public!

Am I A Producer?

What is a producer? A producer of Broadway theater, movies, etc. A producer produces by pulling all the things together; he (or she) hires others to put things together, to paste and glue all the pieces in place.

Am I a producer? Why am I even asking the question? Well, first of all, I could easily define myself as one. I produce weekends, concerts, classes, tours, and special events. I even say in my flier titles: "Jim Gold International presents."

I am also producing the Woodstock Weekend, drawing all the pieces and putting, pasting, placing them together.

I ask myself: Should I hire professionals to do my jobs (like make CDs, books, web designs, take photographs, real recording engineers to record me, etc.) or should I learn to do it all myself?

I'm leaning towards the former. Why? I like what Nikki did on my CD's. She's a real pro, and the CDs look absolutely great. I can be proud of them. I can sell them with pride. This is a good, professional thing.

Seeing myself as a producer elevates the idea of hiring professionals. Sure, I'm pretty good as an amateur, whether it be in web design or CD production, or other. But I'll always be an amateur. It takes years of study, training, and practice to become a true professional. I will never have the time, interest, or energy to become a professional in all these "side" areas. Plus, it is inspiring to work with professionals. They are simply so good. I admire excellence. I love working with excellent people. In fact, working with them is a special treat I could offer myself. It is a personal reward I can give myself. Others might appreciate it too. Not only would I be giving jobs to excellent people, hiring professionals, but I would become inspired in the process.

The idea of Jim Gold Productions also recognizes my skills and talents as an organizer. My organizational skills and talents. I never consider my ability to organize and lead as either a skill or a talent. In fact, I never gave it much thought at all. All my thoughts were, and have been directed towards becoming an artist. Organizational abilities were "side effects" which I naturally possessed. . . like eating or breathing.

Yet they are talents. Not everyone has them. Most people don't recognize their natural abilities. They are so easy and natural, they take them for granted and move on. I am the same way.

Yet, there is no question I have not only leadership abilities, but also organizational skills and talents. Perhaps redefining myself as a "producer" will help me recognize them.

It might also make life richer when I begin to (happily) work with more professionals.

This also means the long "Search to be and become an Artist" phase is coming to an end. Its conclusion: I am an artist. Settled, solved. No problem. End of question.

Now I am ready to move on. To what? Producer. Or better, Producer/Artist. Or even better, Artist/Producer.

I produce a theatrical event, a traveling vaudeville show with my customers as the star players.

My tours are "Traveling Festivals" with each tourist a starring in their own role.

My folk dance classes are stationary theatrical events.

My concert s are a show.

I see all the above as part of a grand constellation of theatrical events, part of the conglomerate Jim Gold Productions.

This is a new, expansive way of looking at things.

This may be the answer to the question: I've done it all. Yes, I've done it all. And I like everything I've done. I can't think of anything new I want to do.

Now, with the new producer approach, I can do it all again, but differently.

The Deepest Road

The deepest road is the road inward. Start traveling today.

How Can I Get My Fee?

Am I confused about my White Plains and Darien folk dance groups? How important are they to me? Where should I go with them?

It is a question of the meaning of money. Money is a motivating force. That is why I partially resent the two groups: I don't make any money with them. But there was always the dream, perhaps rationalization, that some day I would. Also some day group members would register for tours or weekends. And these pay money. This rationalization made teaching a worthwhile part of my business. Plus the classes were a form of advertising, publicity, and promotion.

But if I look at my tour and weekend registration, hardly any of the participants belong to the above groups. Maybe that is the number I can expect.

In any case, I need a new reason to do the above groups. Perhaps my next (and only) challenge is to figure out how to make them pay. $150 a night is a worthwhile fee. How can I get it?

Evidently, I need the above groups because they motivate and challenge me. But now I have to solve the next problem: How can I make money in them? And above that, the general question is: How can I make money teaching folk dancing?

Teaching folk dancing is good for me. I would even say vital. But in order to eliminate the resentment part, I have to figure out a way to make money from it.

Until now I have refused to face the question. I love the field of folk dancing, I love teaching it. But I also have to solve my problem. I need to start asking the big question: How can I make money teaching folk dancing?

Money is a motivator, energizer, and energy source.

Another name for this energy source is "hope."

Chi Running and Company Building

Building JGI: I miss my company building.

Can I apply the principles of Chi Running to company building? To sales, phone calls, advertising, and more. How would that be done?

"What Now?" Spaces

I have finished most of the projects I set out to do this year. My main project was selling this year's tours. . .and this is mostly done. So I face the empty "What now?" spaces.

There is no longer the terrible, vital, gut-wrenching urge to sell, sell, sell. But, on the other hand, it was exciting while it lasted. Selling gave me a new kind of high. I suppose I'd like to continue selling. Besides, what else is there to do?

Sales gave a kind of gone-public meaning to my life. Art gave it a gone-private, imaginative, and in-room meaning.

Sales with its gone-public, and art with its gone-private, are both needed.

Well, we know all this. Where do I go from here?

Could it be that I miss sales, sales are fun, and that I miss my sales fun.

Maybe like the Kantian good-in-itself, sales are fun-in-themselves.

If this is the case, and strangely, I believe it is, then I need something to sell just for the hell of it. Selling is just the game I like play. It energizes me.

Books and Bookings

Maybe it's time for a new direction.

How many times have I and do I say this? Many. Nevertheless, that doesn't make it illegitimate or stupid. Actually, new directions are a daily , "new leaf" occurrence.

So, I repeat: Maybe it's time for a new direction.

Sales, and my life as a salesman will, of course never end. Salesmanship and sales are forever. Nevertheless, my tours sales are on their way and rolling. Even most of next year's 2006 tours are planned.

Perhaps it is time to move on, to expand to other challenges. Such as book and booking sales. Book (and CD) sales are at zero; except for the Klezmer Connection bookings (booked by Michele, not me) booking sales are almost at zero. I put no effort into book or booking sales. Yet, no question, I could make good money at bookings. I especially like the idea of raising my price to $1000 per booking ($900 is good too). Now that's a challenge. And Andrea says the fee is realistic for someone at my level and with specialized talents. I am a specialist. And, like a heart surgeon, they get more money.

Books and bookings are also, like tours, on a national and international level. Of course, folk dance teaching could be, too, especially if I wanted to promote myself in Folk Dance Camps, etc. But they pay little money; also, I've "done" teaching. Sure, I'll take the jobs if they come along. But as far as promoting them, perhaps another time.

I've handled the tour sales challenge successfully this year. I can now expand, use those sales talents, for books and bookings. Perhaps that is my next and new direction.

Re-balancing

Tour sales and the sales personality are here forever. Maybe it is more a question of re-balancing my life.

Maybe cutting back a bit on folk dance teaching (dropping the Darien group, changing Tuesday night to once a month);

Re-balancing the elements in my miracle schedule. "New" place for running, yoga, guitar playing, study, etc.

God

Fun and God

The idea of increasing tour attendance because it is fun leading more people is a new way of looking at tourism.

In the past, I wanted more people on my tours because I would make more money. This is still true. Making more money is always fun. But sheer number, leading more people, as a good-in-itself also brings a higher energy level.

God believes in fun. It's the wonder part of awe-and-wonder. One worships Him *b'simcha*, with joy.

Fun is really joy with a different spelling.

Plus it will be fun making more money, too.

Fun in tourism, the joy of gathering and leading larger groups. More sparks, a greater fire, more energy packettes.

How do I start? First, imagine it.

Total Confidence and Inner Peace

If I live in God's realm, and my decisions, self-image, inner attitudes and concepts all ultimately stem from God, if my doubts about God's power rulership over me have vanished, shouldn't my self doubts vanish with them? Hmmm, why not?

What a delicious new way of looking at self-confidence. It stems from an ultimate belief in God's wisdom and judgement. Putting myself in His hands, I can let go, jump on the railroad train, take the ride, and see where this Conductor will lead me. The illusion is that I am making my decisions. But am I really? Isn't the "I" that seems to make them a mask behind which lies the infinite power of God? His power hurtles through my veins, filling mind, body, and spirit with eternal wisdom and energy.

If I put myself in God's hands, the gift I receive will be total confidence. . .and inner peace.

Above/Within

Above and Within are really the same place.

Have faith in the redeeming power of Above/Within.

Passion and the Bible

It is hard for me to do things in measured, mature, and reasonable fashion. Enthusiasm, passion, and fire are more in tune with my life style. Thus it might be better for me to dive into bible studies with full, all-day force. Passion and fire. Not just a morning study, but morning, afternoon, and evening. . .and even night venture.

I like this.

Prayer, Bible, and Bible Study

Pray three times a day: Jewish style
Morning, afternoon, evening.
Pray five times a day: Moslem style
I could add night. . . and late morning.
How would I pray? By reading, studying, the Torah and Bible. How many times a day? I could start with three. . . or four.

It may mean carrying the Bible on my person. . . at all times. I would bring a Hebrew. . . and Bulgarian version.

Inventions

Paisley T-Bone in a Tither

What fun to piddle and quake. A verbal bug-blast let loose. Ah, to pass time flowing words across the pages, bowling them down the ten-pin alley of letterdom.

Nor is there a way to mechktatize such a boon. In spite of pip-perpassings, the hogtails do continue to swindle.

Keep rolling, oh, oohs. Landlubbers never know the difference. And the stench of centipedes, dripping and follicking their popper ways across nodules of weltfields, do indeed pepper the corns of aching passer buyers.

Can an aching heart really feel the deep entrenchment of loga-rithms? Or must a mathematical plenitude come full swing? Such earthly questions were asked by Lancelot the Third, Fourteen King of Utopia Fifteen.

"Shouldn't I write poop all day?" asked his court grammarian, Paisley Poopensquire. "Or would it be better the poop the deck and leave a leaf at that?"

"Indeed, you dumbwhat turdbone," quoth up Hartley Dunklewickle, corporate leader the Mustard Factory and king of Wienerland. "Accept the truth. Fart at leisure. It will do you good."

"Well, hammer and tong my T-bone," answered Paisley on one knee. "I hadn't consider the mushroom underside of the question. You are right, my fine feather-hammer. I shall stamp on my toe immediately."

Thus did Paisley change his name to the Chinese derivative, Hammer Tong Toe.

Laszlo and his Hungarian computer are leaving Budapest today. The tour of Hortobagy Plainsman is over. Can the plaster nation be far behind?

"Censure is the bottom line of xenophobia," said Bongo Bela as he walked out of his Fathered Gypsy band. "Berkey and Pingy, must go, too. We need tree-love exactitude in the fight against fruithood."

Laszlo leaned against an onion, then hung his head in shame. "Worry not," said Mother Hen, biosphere mama of UNESCO. "The Kyoto environment is headed this way. Japanese are twiting in lemon juice. Once they come, air raids will no longer be in vogue. Then you can peel your character in peace."

"But mother, isn't it dangerous to reveal my secret self in public?"

"Yes, my son, it can be frightening. But for you such revelation is a necessity. It will clear your brain of vacant fodder and will give others a chance to know you."

"Why should they know me, mother? Do I not suffer from internal turniphood?"

"That is exactly why others should know you. It will bring courage and confidence to members of the National Turnip Movement. Life as a vegetable in this world is not easy."

"Thank you, Mama. You have once again fertilized the rubicon workings of my internal vegetable garden and instilled power into my underground cells."

www.ingramcontent.com/pod-product-compliance
Lightning Source LLC
Chambersburg PA
CBHW060834110426
R18122100001BA/R181221PG42736CBX00023BA/19